YA-HONK! GOES THE WILD GANDER

YA-HONK! GOES THE WILD GANDER

or

Covid Divagations

Brian Swann

MADHAT PRESS
CHESHIRE, MASSACHUSETTS

MadHat Press
MadHat Incorporated
PO Box 422, Cheshire, MA 01225

Copyright © 2024 Brian Swann
All rights reserved

The Library of Congress has assigned
this edition a Control Number of
2023950525

ISBN 978-1-952335-71-6 (paperback)

Words by Brian Swann
Cover image and design by Marc Vincenz

www.MadHat-Press.com

First Printing
Printed in the United States of America

For Roberta, as ever

Table of Contents

Proem

The Flag	3
The Pose	4
He	5
The Painting	6
Good News	7
Petals	9
Now You Know	10
The Mirror	11

Part One: The Storm

An Encampment	15
Ducks	16
The Storm	18
The Jay	21
Books	23
Hesdansin	26
Via del Tempio	29
Family	33
Frames	35
Uncle Jack	36
The Scream	38
What's Wrong with Me?	40
The Physical	44
The Other Painting	46
Teeth	48
The Other Side	50
Yob	52
My Sister Eileen	55
The Ladder	57
The Box	60
Jacques Maritain and the Shrew	62
The Contortionist	66
To a Head	67

Modifying the Sahara   68

Part Two: The Fourth Wall

Olive-O or Heptane   73
History   76
The Conqueror   79
The Matter   81
The Morgan   83
That's Life   87
Old Friends   90
These Things Being So   91
Old Clothes   94
Personal   95
Living Lightly with Kierkegaard   97
Work   100
The Window   101
Insect   102
The Garden Center   103
Ontological   104
Invention   106
Mnemonics   107
Keys   111
Avatars   114
Boots   116
The Ukelele   119
Krum Mariste   121
Voice   123
Ghosts   125
At the Museo   126
Nanabush   127
The Universe   128
Recording   130
The Event   132
Enlightenment   137
Coconut Oil   139
Sportsmanship   141

Nowhere	142
Ants	144
Pops	145
The Dog	147
The Case	149
Wimps, or What the Monkey Said	151
House and Garden	154
Structuralism	156
The Egg	159
Cold Feet	161
The Reception	165
Retirement	166
The Fourth Wall	168
Landskip	170
House with Smirr and Luminn	172
A Dream	176
The Castle	179
Graham Bell	181
The Translator	183
Fleas, or The Answer	185
Beyond Milk	187
In the Leaving	189
Painted Lady, or Words in Air	190
The Debate	191
You Never Know	194
Odyssey	195
Beer and Bacon Sandwich	199
Time	201
The Idea of Progress	203
Tintinnabulation	207
Mother Esther of the Murmurations	209
Across the Wide Missouri	212
Acknowledgments	215
About the Author	217

PROEM

The Flag

He, hardly more than a boy, what worlds does he still think he can redeem from way up there? He raises the flag he's woven out of green stuff, blurred hieroglyphics in harsh air, until a sudden downdraft rips it. This time I think he'll come down, but no, he sticks to his swaying perch though now I can sense he's wavering. Maybe now I can tempt him down, save him from himself, he whose skin is no thicker than star-glow. But why would he come down when all I can offer is a world that may not even exist, one I was looking for myself when I came upon him, the boy up there with his flag in tatters battling a growing gale? I almost hope he won't come down.

The Pose

He sits atop a heap of coke and clinker, fly ash and slag. All around, broken wings, severed feet, feathers, cogs and wheels of machines, old and new, a flower, a hand sans fingers, fingers sans hands, hands sans everything. One of his hand's a stump. The other might still manage its work of touch, stretch a blessing. If he could make a tear his one good eye would fill, but the world would be a blur. If he tries to rise he'd find he is no bird. He holds his broken pinions out, parchment brittle. He is no longer beautiful though in him beauty still burns with a heatless slow flame. As he waits to be consumed, he keeps his poise, more resolute than doubt. He holds it all together with a pose, the one-eyed angel atop a smoldering pile.

He

thought he was going somewhere. He went somewhere but it wasn't where he thought he wanted to go, and when he arrived it was as if he hadn't because you can't remember the future the way you can the past which is, for instance, a face you once had in a photo you rejected. Yes, he wanted to be left alone, free of images, to sleep and know that when he woke he would still be sleeping.

The Painting

Today I woke again with nothing to go on, no evidence, no clues. No one knows what's coming and even if a cure arrives there may be no one left to save. But I am getting ahead of myself. The good thing is, I suppose, that I'm alive, and there is something for me to go on, there flat against the wall, my painting. I look at its amorphous sky-blue shapes floating, quite still, just whatever they are, no more, going nowhere. If they could go, where would they go? They'd be just as likely to fall flat on the floor as investigate space where their lack of dimension would quickly become apparent. They'd learn that falling feels a lot like flying until you hit the ground where their blue would mean nothing to the brown wood floor. I hope my gaze keeps them afloat.

Good News

I look at the sky carefully, and as I look the quicksilver face clouds over. In its place a sheet of wind moves like water down a plate of glass behind which swallows circle, scatter, circle again as if not quite sure until, sure, they set off headlong into the blue, the whole world theirs. I go inside to consult my calendar with its Poor Richard mottoes stressing moderation, delaying pleasure, playing it safe. Though it's almost April, snow starts to fall. I look out on a land soon to be fantastical, theatrically blurred in all directions. Bodhidharma stared at a blank wall until he saw nothing. Hugh of St. Victor said "he is perfect for whom the entire world is as a foreign land," so when I took off in a series of expanding flights and lost contact with my base I wasn't worried. I felt perfect. Light bent around me and reunited on the other side like water round a boulder in a stream for light doesn't travel in a straight line, it travels by the quickest path. And this light made me "invisible" which is only a way of paralyzing the attention. I decided I was always in the middle because there is no beginning and no end there. Also, misinformation is more important than information since it leads into rich detours. Anyhow, tapping out the melodic code to whoever was tuned in, I went on my way until by mid-afternoon I'd grown feathery thighs and sprouted stubby wings. Talking myself through, I captured the blue in the prism all round me and used it to take close-ups of creatures of light, reflecting more light despite the late hour and the fact that it all seemed to have happened before, and would no doubt happen again. Suddenly I had no idea where I was, feeling myself going on and on, spreading myself thin until adjustments became distractions. Where was I? Why? Almost at once I was back on the ground, dragging my shadow in dust. I was as plain as a line of wind on water, saying *Everything is Everywhere*. And that's what I reported to anyone who would listen. I told them the good news, to free them up, but even as I spoke the words were ephemeral as air, invisible as music, the way in memory the mundane becomes marvelous.

Petals

All night two notes see-sawed, sometimes near, sometimes far, a plucked pipa, a bird I'd never heard before, fooled by the full moon to think dawn, until I rise to the world, spreading its luminous shadow through which a plane slips, self-contained with cushions, attendants, even a place to leave your waste that flies around with you.

In full sun, by the pond I turn around to a beam of shimmering motes in which an astronaut is floating about with something that broke off and which he's trying to fix, never doubting the importance of his mission, his place in the larger scheme of things, or his ability to fix anything so we can live among the stars or play on the moon, be someone else enfolding phantoms, embracing emanations.

But now here I am bent over the pond in September heat, waiting and watching, looking for dimensions in which to fully wake, even if, frustrated, I touch my image, breaking up so I'm everywhere in bits, drifting out, coming back, pleats in parasols, drifting partners of receding dreams, petals of a continual drowning.

Now You Know

—the Vale of Soul-making

From little holes in the ground light seeps up, filtering into flowers and flares I try to gather even if at my touch they collapse to dust or precipitate out.

Sometimes I think I could turn ponds over and streams around, sky backwards and inside out, always on the lookout for something else, as if I could distinguish dust from fallout on the fractured shape of things, looking for a world self-explanatory, the way a tree is, not the way a dream fools you into thinking it needs help, calling you in then springing the trap.

And something else, yes, as I stand watching the tide labor over mud with a cargo of detritus so strange it looks new, how a healthy immune system might look in a pandemic, laden but not overwhelmed. Wind from the hinterland pushes against it with pulses that could be deeper inside you, other breaths in each of the body's cells, wings flapping overhead in silence featureless as a pebble until a gull's shadow leaves the flock, angles in for a moment, cuts across, and is lost against sky's skeins. I stand among shadows sumptuous even on stone, listen to a murmur like small birds rising, watch in the distance a hawk bank, turn and will swoop, making it hard to breathe. But I breathe, here where I am.

I wondered where I was going.
Now I know.

The Mirror

My earliest memory is alone, age about five, in the middle of the night, waking and sitting up to find myself staring into the long mirror at the foot of the bed, seeing nothing. I screamed. I screamed.

Now, as I move into my eighth and in all likelihood final decade, I realize an empty mirror doesn't have to be terrifying. After all, Nirvana has often been compared to an empty mirror, a mirror that no longer reflects objects. So I join E. M. Cioran in his toast: "To a mirror, then, forever pure, forever unemployed."

Part One: The Storm

An Encampment

This usually fast-moving, noisy, crowded, rushing city was quiet, virtually deserted except for police cars and ambulances rushing up 1st Avenue, "Bedpan Alley," named for its number of hospitals. What people there were wore masks and kept apart from each other. Some were heading home laden with toilet paper, some were pushing carts filled with pallets of toilet rolls. As we walked down the avenue we saw that the homeless and mentally disturbed, who previously had been largely camouflaged if not unseen, were now fully visible, slouching on corners, sitting by cardboard messages, standing vacant in vacant shopfronts with empty grocery carts filled with whatever they had. There was the beginning of a homeless encampment on the corner of 1st and 15th, under a construction awning. A man was writing in chalk on the sidewalk, while another was scratching away on a sheet of old plywood.

Ducks

I write in longhand with stubs of HB pencils. I use the back of paper already used. I can't throw anything away. Over and over I scribble in old-fashioned cursive, piling up palimpsests. If I try erasing it's no longer with real rubber but hi-polymer, which works even worse.

For years I've kept these pencils pointed with a pearl-handled penknife handed down generations. From time to time I use a machine whose shavings give off something of the pine scent I've loved since a boy when I climbed into pine branches to lose myself. I keep these stubs in the deep cluttered recesses of my antique maple desk. When another stub is needed I feel about blindly the way we used to catch catfish by the tail, under the bank.

I also use the penknife to scrape shapes into the desk's old, venerable, deep waxed surface. I make a long landscape complete with walls and towers and a sky of stars and figures, comets and streaks. Each day the desk grows with more land and sky, a sea with boats, a sailing ship whose deck is collapsing. At first, you can hear nothing. Then the gunwale caves in, the hull groans and cracks. Soon fingers are clutching at whatever they can, but it is all slippery as fish. Then the switchboard lights up in a number of directions, hopeless headlights reach into night trying to predict what will loom up next, but they keep snagging on helpless birds, stars brittle as chandeliers. You try to make yourself heard above the breakers, the rumble of shoals as you're driven onto rocks. You're swamped. You hold your breath, until in the far northeast quadrant two ducks appear, male and female. They fly out of the scene and into the pool at the center of our complex. The fountain splashes as they paddle round, probably refugees from the East River, an arrow's flight away. This area before the pandemic was usually filled with nannies and babies, children running, playing, kicking balls, scooting scooters. Now it is almost empty, just three or four people on benches keeping "social distance". Besides the fountain splashes, the only sound is the constant wail of ambulances floating over rooftops. Why are the ducks here? A sign says "Don't feed the wildlife." They don't seem to worry where their next meal is coming from as they paddle about. *Look at us,* they seem to say. *Watch us. Do what we do.* A woman gets up from the bench, walks over and takes a photo with her phone.

Brian Swann

The Storm,

that dreadful pother, seems to come from two directions, in from the East River and up from the Lower East Side. I stare out through the glass at thrashing London plane trees and oaks planted at the end of World War II in what had been the Gaslight district. I'd watched those trees come to life each spring, their yellow-green tips rising closer to my 8th-floor windows. Now I had the urge to reach out and touch them, climb out into the trees themselves, then, to distant thunder and lashing rain, I was back at a small dinner at Princeton where James Baldwin was the guest of honor. He was angry, smacking the table hard, screaming "She's gotta pee! She's gotta pee!" still, years later, humiliated at the NJ gas-station attendant refusing to let his sister use the bathroom. Then I was at a table in Alabama, silent while Mr. Rushton, Princeton alum, President of Provident Life Insurance in Birmingham, put me to rights, informing me that those "so-called Civil Rights workers" were screwing in churches, that the man or men who dynamited "that Negro Baptist Church with the little girls" were "one of their own", and that Martin Luther King lined his own pockets with thousands if not millions out of "those protests."

This trance is interrupted by the occupant of 9B directly overhead doing her best to drown out the rain and thunder with extra vigorous and persistent application of frequent apartment cleaning, searching out and scouring every stray Covid virus she could find. Furniture is being rolled around, back and forth, a machine sounding like an earth mover shakes the ceiling, a steam-roller trundles slowly around accompanied by a maddening array of thumps, scratchings and scrapings like giant rats or squirrels trapped in the walls. This happens in each of her rooms and once finished soon begin again, at all different times, a.m. and p.m., unpredictably. Yes, the lock-down is clearly taking its toll on our upstairs neighbor, the reclusive medical researcher Dr. A. who is now extra reclusive and has taken to snaking her toilet three or four times a day. Her mother had visited from Bangladesh a few years ago and spent hours each day pashing and pummeling cloth in the bathtub, water flowing constantly and once coming through the ceiling to flood our apartment. This was the lady who, when phoning the Indian subcontinent, opened the window and yelled in a voice that had no need of a phone. We had had to call the police more than once because someone, who turned out to be a niece Dr. A. had loaned her apartment to, when not yowling in orgasm was racing up and down the corridor screaming she was being raped, or murdered, or both. Now the storm has abated a bit, giving me more space to think how the neighbors on our floor are reacting to the Covid crisis. In 8A, the family is extra silent, as if the quieter they are the less chance there is of their being targeted. The husband no longer pings his awful piano and the wife only opens the door just wide enough to have supplies delivered, then closes it, fast. There is no evidence of the teenage daughter. 8C is silent because the occupant died five months ago, and her accountant son who lives in Brooklyn has decided, for whatever reason, to keep paying the rent. Across the hall, 4F is also silent, the dentist and his family having decamped for their place in the Hamptons, while in 8G the psychotic has placed even more notices on her door declaring she will never open it for anyone under any circumstances. Packages stack against her door until she retrieves them. 8E is occupied by two young Chinese girls who yesterday managed to start a fire in their oven that required half a dozen firemen to put out, having first spent time persuading one of the girls to let them in after she claimed she had just taken a shower and was naked. "You need to open the door," one of the men said. "We won't look. Wear your mask." 8D, where an elderly lady had jumped from a window, is now full of young people who party a lot.

The Jay

I have been puzzling over (1) why, after scrambling over loose shingles and looser roof tiles in danger of falling, he arrived back at the place he was escaping, and (2) why then, with his pursuers on the look-out and planning his capture, he jumped from roof to garden wall and flew off to freedom, a screeching blue jay, and they didn't even notice. Now, a blue jay is a crow, *corv*us, and as St. Augustine wrote: *dormio, et cor meum vigilat*, "I sleep, and my heart awakens." So I ask myself, is it any wonder that my heart awakens to the person who eludes his would-be captors by transforming himself before their very eyes, eyes which were clearly shut to the possibility of transformation? I also ask, unrelated, or very loosely related, to the above, (3) why can't I remember the proper name of the Viking king who commanded the waves to retreat—actually, he did what he did to show sycophantic courtiers the limits of his power? I kept calling him "Midas" as if he could turn the tide to gold which, in a sense, it already is with its depths and weight of commerce. I was thinking all the above after a day when I was forced to go out and visit the bank (hence, no doubt, Midas), not at all sure I'd be able to access funds which I may not, in any case, be able to use to any extent since almost all the stores were shut and boarded up. In any event, I did go out, home-made mask up to my eyes like a yashmak, jigging and side-stepping so as not to come within six feet of anyone. Of course, when I got to the bank, it was closed, with a guard outside who would not answer questions. People milled about, angry, so angry I felt they might turn on me, chase me, so I left and made my way back home, glasses steaming up from breath trapped under the cloth mask. I felt faint, having forgotten to take my Ramipril. My chest began an irregular rhythm, heart flipping. I had a toothache. Dentists were closed. Something was creeping up on me. I wished I could fly. I managed to make it back and switch on TV, only to find reports of people defying stay at home orders and social distancing, protests citing 1st, 2nd, whatever, amendments allowing them to do whatever they wanted in the name of freedom. Someone blocked the camera with a sign that said *Let My People Go*. A truck rolled by with *GOD is my vaccine* painted on the side, and I thought, if God is the vaccine then he must also be the virus, but who would want to paint that on the side of a truck? I felt helpless. If only my heart would wake, I thought, or at least calm down, and then I might be able to do something to help, something that would make sense, but I couldn't even remember my doctor's name, let alone my cardiologist's or the name of that king until—there, I had it! Canute, really "Knut," "King Knot," his parents had had enough children and intended to call a stop, tie a knot in it. I knew how they felt, in spades. Call it quits. Fly away.

Books

The mind shrinks like a sun-dried raisin, too. It flips. I read that people are reporting very, very strange dreams, perhaps the mind trying to cheat the virus by creating its own reality, tell stories like Scheherazade, to trick the tyrant into a change of heart. So here we are together, sheltering in place and, if one can use such a word in such circumstances, happy. Sheltering in place in fact plays right into our hands. We were built for this, our society of two, connected to the world by an old wallphone, rejecting the i-phone. For some years we have lived in the middle of Manhattan as if we were in a hut in deepest Alaska. Now Roberta reads a lot and generously always invites me to "dip into" any book she is reading, mostly novels, and I do though, as she knows, I don't care for reading and fiction is not my favorite mode. But yes, a toe here, a finger there, I dip in, sometimes even a whole foot or hand. She knows my first reaction to anything is negative, but she also knows that a nudge or two from her will often change my mind. This is how I developed a wardrobe, moving from L.L. Bean shirts, boots and jeans to a whole range of shirts, socks, coats, even slacks, though jeans are still my staple. She's been at me a few days now, quietly persistent, to share a book she's taken with. Finally, "you never give up, do you?" I say. She looks at me. "Where would we be if I'd given up on you all those years ago?" she inquires. "You have lots of books," I say, trying to change the subject. "Tons. I love you." I look around the room, books filling shelves and stacked against walls. "I'm going to need them," she notes, and in fact in this pandemic she has proven right and continues to try to persuade me to share her wealth, leaving books open all over the place, dropped as if by accident on my side of the bed, on the sofa, on the floor. This morning I found on my desk a bulky tome with a note: "Just in case you'd like to dip in, you obstinate, foot-stamping monkey." Now she has gone to the trouble of trying to trick me with non-fiction, so I clear off my papers, sit down and flip through a book about how literature saved the author's life, though it turned out that the whole point was that in spite of all his efforts it didn't. The last paragraph said the author's loneliness was not "assuaged" by literature since nothing can affect the human condition. "Language," he added, "does not save anyone's life." I could have told him this before he started out on his trek. In fact, the book turned out to be really an excuse to list everything compulsively: so many books read, a catalog of names and dropping of same, from Nobel prizewinners to former students who went on to great things, stuff he'd written and stuff he wished he'd written, how to play the electric guitar, Luther, Lethem, Lawrence, Borges, *Amadeus*, Larry David, Yankees, Pascal, Wallace, Coetzee et al., all to prove "we live in a culture that is completely mediated and artificial." I could have told him that too, that it's the human condition, because "mankind everywhere has always been creative," as the great anthropologist Franz Boas said. And I could also have told him that this pandemic feels neither mediated nor artificial, and where nothing feels fixed, everything evolving and up for grabs, how is one to write about it? There's maybe a clue from my late anthro friend Catherine McClellan who told me that in Tlingit stories mythical actions blend with behaviors of ancestors and relatives, solemn and cosmological weave in with vulgar and hilarious; so-called "categories" collapse. But there again I just saw a picture of a Covid-19 being, at once tiny, simple and complex, a mysterious unconscious working mind of structural proteins and replicating RNA. What does it want, and why? What does it mean? And how do you deal with that?

Hesdansin

Indoors over a month, with a short excursus to the bank, another to the post office, and a daily short walk by myself followed by a longer walk with Roberta. Despite the constant closeness of a two-bedroom apartment, there's only been one disagreement over who-knows-what, and that resolved quite quickly though it seemed to be rooted in events of long ago, long thought concluded and forgotten. Apparently, nothing is ever really resolved, especially in circumstances where one is forced inward, backward, deep, and where memory is a way of staying connected, even when one doesn't want to be connected to everything in one's life. Now, panic is never very far away. I am beginning to get chest pains, or I think I am. One needs to do something, anything; it's time to effect things long put off such as house cleaning and reordering one's surroundings, including the place where I write this, once a study lined with bookshelves but now a storehouse for items transported from the country house we sold four years ago. It is also a pantry piled with extra food in case of the worst. Getting to my desk is an adventure in itself. But improving this room has proven largely impossible, so Roberta has changed the cushions in the living room, thrown a new cover over the armchair, swapped out the duvee in the bedroom, dumped old cutlery and replaced it with a real silver set we'd hoarded for ever, keeping for what? For some time we'd planned to do a laundry, in compliance with the new Covid laws fixed to the laundry room door. But the stuff piled up and instead of taking care of it we did something else, in my case deciding to clean out one of my filing cabinets, in the process of which I came across some notes I was going to use for something or other. At the time I wrote them, I was in New Mexico and riding each day at the Lobo Ranch near Taos.

"Whiskey" was my mount, if "mount" you could call him, a good-natured roan who kept stopping to bite off oak seedlings and small trees, pausing to admire the scenery. It always ended up with my dismounting and walking ahead as if I was walking the dog. Whiskey followed as he saw fit, or not. Sometimes I followed him. The only time he broke from a stop-and-start stroll was when we were nearing his barn and I had to preserve appearances by climbing aboard. Off he galloped downhill with me hanging on as best I could. Now, I grew up across from a small farm and spent a lot of time with its horses, even sleeping with them in the straw. I was never comfortable with the man/animal formula. I've always felt more comfortable around animals than humans; trees too, for that matter. As *Monty Python*'s Terry Gilliam said, "I'll worship a tree any day. Give me a nice stream I'll worship that." But I digress. Let us return to those notes I found concerning a 7-year-old claustrophobic, manic-depressive bay racehorse named Hesdansin, whose grandfather was the great Nijinsky. He'd been quite normal until weaned and separated from his mother, which was when he began galloping round his stall. They'd hung two snow tires from the rafters to slow him down, but next morning he'd be covered with treadmarks. They tried a pet goat, Jerry, to calm him down, but next morning they were both running round. They painted his stall pink since his owner had been told that manic-depressive horses loved that color. Next morning she had a pink horse. She hung a large mirror hoping he'd see what he was doing and would stop. He looked over his shoulder into the mirror as he sped by. Clearly, as a racehorse, though talented he was useless. He was exhausted most of the time. But he's doing fine, spending his days outside under a large umbrella for hot days and with plenty of blankets for cold nights. He also has a black cat with the unlikely name of Brian for company. His only drawback is that he's still Hesdancin and likes to eat the umbrellas. He's on his fifth.

Via del Tempio

Everything shrinks, but limits induce pleasure. Each day we sit on the bed and watch Cuomo's Covid update while we eat lunch, often exotic items Roberta has provided magically from her brief shopping outings. We walk round our complex, often to the East River, or we sit on a bench and talk. After forty-five years we still have a lot to say. Then, back in the apartment, she reads and I sit at my desk writing, or trying to write, or scavenging journals from way back before we met, wandering around in worlds where times seems almost arbitrary, worlds that now seem impossible, in other galaxies shining as I turn brittle pages, like these here now, still stained with Tiber mud after everything I owned was stolen and when discovered to be worthless, tossed into the river. *River* makes me look up and out the window, think about those two ducks that visited our fountain from the East River, what they meant, what I could make them mean, wondering how long they'll hang around, if they will—. I drop my eyes back to the page where in Edward's dark room Ursula is sitting on the floor making a bikini from the brand-tags she'd cut from men's ties, pullovers, shirts. She's a Swedish model for *Foto Romanza*, making twenty thousand lire a day. Last episode, she was a maid accused of stealing but ended up marrying the family's eldest son, a doctor. When she isn't making bikinis she knits, yellow wool on yellow plastic needles, sipping tonic water, popping pills for her thyroid condition, pills that cost, she says, twenty-eight thousand lire, so she has to work a lot. She never eats but nibbles from our plates, "just to try it," but once, she tells us, she ate a wheel of Dutch cheese by herself, all at one sitting. I turn pages and come across lunch at Da Giggetto across the street from our apartment in the ghetto, near the synagogue. Little Leroy is drawing on the paper tablecloth. No one knows how Jose became Little Leroy. When I first arrived, he cleaned my room, which contained only a bed. He offered to wash my underwear and wrote down the Italian for "sheets," then took me to the room he shared with Graham. We listened to his Brazilian records and he offered to teach me Portuguese. When I declined his offer of coffee, he was upset. To escape, I went to the bathroom. He followed and told me how to work the lock. I returned to my room, which had no lock, when I heard the dreaded carpet-slipped shuffle. "You want tea then?" "No." "You strange. All English like tea." He asked me why I was in Rome, how I met Edward ("he ran from Viet Nam, he has a 'libretto' so he can't drive a car, or marry"), how much money I made from teaching. I took a deep breath. "You don't like conversation?" he asked. I gave him a cigarette which he tucked behind his ear "for Graham." He told me about his mother, divorced and living in Bolzano, then ran out and returned with a glass of anise liquor. "It's lonely here," he said. "I miss my mother and she misses her unique son. Do you like your moustache?" He brought me a blanket. The window was half open. He opened it. "No one sleep in open window," he said. "No one." He shuffled off. "I'm only twenty." I heard a scream, and found him in the kitchen, distressed at discovering his underpants all holes after he'd put them to steep in toilet bleach. And now here we are at Da Giggetto, in the front room, the place reserved for locals, while the likes of Fellini and other celebrities dine at the rear. Leroy is drawing on the paper tablecloth. He snares pieces of my cheese and bits of Graham's lamb. He asks Pamela for a kiss, but she refuses. She is angry at him. "No, I will not give you a kiss." That morning he'd taken her shopping. She'd said that on the way she was going to learn Italian by reading every sign out loud and Leroy had to correct her if she made a mistake. But when he did correct her she lost her temper and they argued. By the time they got to the supermarket it was closed. Furious and hot, she decided to return home but, too tired to walk, she tried to clamber aboard the first bus she saw and Leroy had to haul her off. But then she waddled off on her strong white legs to catch the next bus she saw. She was surprisingly quick and, despite Leroy trying to convince her the bus was going in the wrong direction, she hopped aboard before he could catch her and he was forced to follow. The bus was crowded, Pamela was trampled and jostled. When she finally found a seat she was hysterical. By the time they got back home she was in a filthy temper. The apartment lock was broken, and there was a special way to open it, but Pamela just put her hefty Cockney shoulder to it and it flew open, depositing her inside, with an anxious Leroy on top of her. "Now we won't be able to open or shut the door," he said. "Shut up, you!" she yelled, dashing into the bathroom. "Graham's mother is one big complicated woman," Leroy said to me that evening, recounting this tale. "I wouldn't want to marry her. Is your mother like that? She give me square balls, triangle balls, square square balls." And now, late afternoon, Graham, exhausted from one of his private English lessons, is in the tub. Little Leroy, in shorts with white spots trimmed with white lace, is washing his back. Pamela is sitting on the side of the becrudded toilet. The bathroom lock is broken, the door is open. In the handbasin, the hot tap doesn't work and the cold tap can't be turned off. It drips into the sink green with moss. The windows are cracked or shattered and a cool breeze from Ostia blows through. Graham is shivering in the shallow water that had been heated in pans on the kitchen stove. The unwashed plates that had been piled in the bathtub are scattered on the floor along with a scuffed-up pair of high-heel shoes, a couple of balled-up skirts and some blouses. Pamela labors to her feet, picks up the blouses, carries them down the corridor to Edward's room where she tosses them onto his bed among dresses, balled-up skirts and blouses and an open empty handbag. Sanitary napkins and garter belts sit next to a home cocktail set. Then she goes to Graham's room, which he shares with Leroy and now with her. The blinds are always drawn. Propped against the wall on top of the dresser is a card Leroy had sent from Bolzano, a mare with her foal: "The big hors its you and a little hors its me. I love you." From the bathroom I hear, "I won't stay here another five minutes! I don't care if you never come home again! This is the last time I visit. You may be my own son but I want nothing more to do with you." Then silence. "And you, you little twerp, shut up! Graham was fine until he met you, and that Edward, and all those girls." Two days before, Pamela had come across Ursula and Little Leroy in the bathroom. He claimed he was just cutting her eyelashes. Graham had been teasing him unmercifully. The apartment door opened, then slammed shut. "No," Pamela tells Leroy, "I will not give you a kiss."

Family

Today on TV I watched the burial of bodies in boxes on Ward Island in the Bronx, the place where unclaimed bodies end up. Not for the first time it occurred to me that this could be my fate, still a stranger in a strange land. With so much time on my hands, as I said, I've been going through old journals, yellowing files, scraps of paper and old letters. Today I found something I'd totally forgotten, part of a letter I must have written to myself and never mailed, concerning my father's family, something he told me on my last visit over 40 years ago. I never knew his parents. I only knew that he hated his father, the cause in 1923 of his walking, age 14, five miles from Cambridge to the Royal Navy recruiting office in Great Shelford. While he was abroad, his mother, whom he loved, died. I recall him weeping, he who never cried and whose main emotion was anger. I know little about his family, though one of his grandparents, I believe, was named Alice O'Neill, born in Cork and left a widow at 23 with two young children. Somehow she ended up in Cambridge, where she worked as a cook, perhaps at a college. I have also heard tell of another relative who worked as a gardener at Queens' College where, many years later, I became a student, and a story about a great-great-grandfather who was a carpenter on an estate in Saffron Walden. He was a practical joker, one of whose tricks involved his wife (as I recall, they all seemed to involve his wife). It went as follows: She went into the outhouse to relieve herself. Now in those days this facility was merely a hole with a plank across. Great-great-grandmother went into the dark but didn't notice that her husband was pushing a clothes prop slowly through a hole in the door. Next thing the poor woman knew she'd been tipped backwards, skirts over her head. The cries and screams of the good church-going woman could be heard right up to the mansion itself. And that charming story is all I know about my father's side of the family. I know a bit more of my mother's who, so far as I know, are also all gone.

Frames

I have fallen asleep in another country. Saturday night, in the black-out. Through the window you can make out a boy in what's left of the family's weekly hot bath water. The air-raid siren drones *All Clear*. He pulls the plug, sits shivering as water drains leaving a tide-mark. Fade, then bring up a time-lapse collage of archival footage, search-lights, house-fires and so on, ending with people we think we recognize but can't be sure, a young woman cutting herself, a man knocking back pints, a woman who could be his mother, staring at the camera, knitting, and so on, while slowly into focus comes a wind-bent tree, a long line of eiders crossing empty sand, a boy on his knees scrying rock pools, then the tide retreating, opening the causeway to Lindisfarne's sand hills where he sends crabs with lit candles on their backs down burrows to scare out conies he chases but can't catch. Fade, then bring up gray and a sound like glaciers grinding. Slow focus on a man at his door, looking into distant mountains, long white hair loose. Fade with a brant's call, gull's screech, fisher lassie's call: *"Caller herring, caller herring, who'll buy my fresh herring?"*

Uncle Jack

The elevated highway we're driving on runs right round the city. We have to drive slowly, not only because it is narrow and crowded with people but also because the Mister Softee ice-cream truck we're towing is a bit loose and wobbles. We'd just passed a large garbage container with what looks like a family inside celebrating a haul of plates, cups, saucers and other assorted domestic items, when Uncle Jack decides to squeeze between two empty roll-on-and-off dumpsters. We make it through but, with a screech of metal on metal Mister Softee gets stuck. Uncle Jack cuts the engine and gets out to consider the situation. "We could push it back out the way we came," he says, only to nix the idea. "Or maybe we could go back round and shove it through," he emends. "Or maybe we could get someone, or something, to pull one of the dumpsters to the side and make just enough room for us to squeeze through." That too is rejected as impractical since we don't know anybody round here. Uncle Jack scratches his chin and quickly withdraws his hand on which there is a speck of blood. "I have an idea," he says. "Let's retrace our steps and reconsider from a different perspective." Which is what we do. We get back in, he starts the engine and puts the truck in reverse. With a squealing and scratching we slowly begin moving backwards, Uncle Jack twisting round to look through the rear window. As he does so, sunlight hits his right cheek and I catch a flash of light from bits of glass that still from time to time work their way to the surface from when he drove his motorcycle over the cliffs at Tynemouth onto rocks and into the sea. Soon we decide Mr Softee is more hindrance than help so we cut him loose. Now we are off the highway, traveling faster backwards than forwards. People jump aside like crickets. Everything flashes by until we come to a traffic island, "roundabout" as we used to call them. "How's this going to help?" I wonder, but Uncle Jack is my favorite uncle and I trust him. When I was a baby he used to put me in the large top drawer in the living room by the fire and pretend I'd disappeared. It is still a cherished childhood memory.

The Scream

I've been sitting at my desk so long even my nerves have long shadows. If I were to greet you it would sound cryptic or circumspect. I turn to see on the silent TV screen someone sitting at a desk, writing longhand. He goes on for some time. It is not much of a plot.

So I sit here thinking about thinking, how I am my remembered thought and any experiencing self that does my living is like a stranger to me and I cannot remember who said that, certainly not me, and how one possesses oneself in flashes and how suicide is an extreme form of self-fascination and how another person becomes a cast of characters and how I hate actors because what kind of a world is it when people can spend their entire lives as others? no, I think, there is no self so what does it mean when Dogen Zenji says that to know the self is to forget the self and to forget the self is to be enlightened? no, I think, the way to get through this life is to treat yourself as a foreigner and the world as foreign, as the 12th-century mystic Hugh of St. Victor said, and to write, as Henri Michaux said, as if from a foreign land ("je vous écrit d'un pays lointain"), but what would I write, especially in a tongue I don't know? maybe Adorno's spiderwebs or a starfish's regenerative limbs or the glass sponge's intricate mesh of silica capable of withstanding high stress, or, all art aspiring to the condition of music, write in the medium of breath Schubert's Nocturne for Piano Trio in E flat major, or—yes, good luck with that I say, getting to my feet and sitting back down. Not much of a plot. So here I sit with few feelings for things and fewer for others. Whenever I think I can see their souls, it is just them with no clothes on. For me, presence is a less likely form of absence, as when you walk in winter woods and flush quail so they scare you and vanish, or when, on a city street pre-Covid, someone you bump says "Who the hell do you think you are?" As if you knew. And I sit here gazing through the darkening window and up into space where there are ladders going everywhere, all sorts of ladders against all sorts of walls, or no walls at all, and behind that a path climbing a hill and a giant's paternoster voice booming out threats, telling you where to go, what to do, as if you are only a formula, and a scream.

"How can you think such things?" a female voice asks. "But if you believe you heard a scream you heard a scream, or enough to know what a scream is." This, I muse, is where the gods come in. If you only think you hear them, you hear them. You can't undo them. At worst they are an echo, what's left over for you to pull together.

Meanwhile, I've been sitting at my desk so long I don't know where I am. All round me drags on; things have retreated into their shadows. Multiples flow into one dim lamp. Lonely men find old bones, one stick to make a fire. I look out the dark window, heavy with the stuff of stones. It's now pointless to look in the mirror for confirmation; it's a model of emptiness. Still, if you look long enough something might emerge from among—there, across the way, beside the house with all the curtains drawn and lights out, another house like this one but as if filled with snow, and from snowbanks all round a scream, or something like a scream, and again, the noise, the echo emptiness makes.

What's Wrong with Me?

An elderly homeless woman sits with her back to the CVS store. A cardboard sign says she is homeless and needs help. "Good morning, sir," she says. "Fuck off," I say under my breath. What's wrong with me?

Back home, I ask the same question. I blame Ubu-Trump. I blame the virus. To take my mind off what might be an unpleasant truth about myself, always blaming others, I go to my study, walk over to the old filing cabinet, pull out a file at random. It falls to the floor. "All thumbs," I say to myself. "What's wrong with me?" Strange phrase, "all thumbs," I think. I boot up my laptop and google the phrase. "Clumsy," it says, "awkward." I knew that. What else? I look at the file on the floor. "All Thumbs" is written on it. Strange. I pick it up and put it on the desk. More on this later. I go to another file, very thin. "Travels," it says. I'm not even sure I wrote what I read. Not my style. "SECRET CAVES on billboards twenty feet high," I read. "Rooms you can't stay in and can't wait to get out of. Last night the cry of a fox was so fierce it could have been the only fox in the world looking for another one. In the village store they're discussing details of the latest fire. Daddy's Girl asks Gene, Anybody get burned, like? Momma comes from behind the mailboxes to make a BLT for no one in particular. A ways down the road, crews widen Route 8 into a three-laner. One car passes all day. In fields that look scraped raw, farmers on tractors go through the motions. Holsteins, jaws moving as one, hedge their bets, some standing, some lying. Woman after woman parades along the shoulder going from here to there and back again, so fat their Bermuda shorts seem another person. *For Sale* signs are everywhere." I read it over again, this time aloud. I don't like it. No empathy. I need cheering up, Ah, a "Comedy/Joke" file. What have we here? "A group of five potty-mouthed parrots have been separated at a British zoo because of incessant swearing. Billy, Eric, Elsie, Jade and Tyson were moved to different locations after officials determined they were imitating each other using the F-bomb and other swear words. 'We're quite used to parrots swearing,' said a zoo official, 'but for some reason these five relish it.' The parrots were moved so that kids didn't hear the foul language, although adults enjoyed it."

This lifts my mood. I return to the cabinet, reach in for another file which happens to be "Childhood and Youth." I find a sheet with "Broda" penciled on top on top. Broda? Ah, Paul, my friend, yes. I began reading how his mother was our primary school doctor who embarrassed us by cupping our balls and making us cough. A spy herself, she was married to the atom spy Alan Nunn May, Paul's stepfather. Poor Paul, his real father, Engelbert, had also been a Soviet spy. I continued, reading about our high school Combined Cadet Force on its annual camp among the army regulars in Thetford. One day, there was a commotion outside one of the tents. Cadets had grabbed Paul, stripped him, and covered him with the dubbin used on gaiters and belts. When they had finished, he stood up, walked past laughing onlookers slowly and with great dignity across the parade ground to the showers. That was all. What I hadn't written down was that I had said and done nothing. What was wrong with me, even then? Years later, I found out that Paul had become a distinguished microbiologist. I felt like a microbe.

But back to that "All Thumbs," which from internal evidence seems to have been written in the early days of the web. The writer evinces a sense of humor which I feel somewhat absent from his present manifestation as me. Yes, he doesn't seem to have had much wrong with him, unless you count writing poems about porn. Ah, libido, even in a comic vein. Another thing wrong with me now is lack of libido. I blame this too on Trump and the pandemic. I haven't been to a gym in ages. From twenty "All Thumbs," I pick one from the exact middle:

Thumb X

In our gym this would get you thrown out—
they almost threw me out for not showering before a swim
and for not wearing a cap, after a final warning
for not wiping down the equipment after use.
Yet there *are* naked girls in my gym, though they have to be
under four to get in the changing room,
and be accompanied by their daddies. Anyhow,
these shirtless and topless girls are buff.
He must have trained them well. Certainly,
one has no problem lifting his dumbbell.
She's generous too. *Here,* she says to the other girl,
*you can lift this too. I'll help you. There. Mmm.
Thanks. There's enough to go round.* Now,
as I think I said, this kind of thing couldn't happen
in our gym of alterkakers, sour women, middle-aged men
with their first child, the occasional foul-mouthed adolescent,
and me. This gym here is squeaky clean, empty too,
except in the corner with a line of gleaming barbells,
the trio, and a wide-open window.
It must be summer, or spring.

Yes, what's wrong with me? Yesterday, I walked past two signs in a store window: "Psychic Boutique," and "Psychic Readings, Love Life, Health, Finances." The future being hazy,

I was tempted to go in, except the place was boarded up. I did go to a psychic once, a Jungian, who detected all sorts of archetypes in me and predicted a long life which has proved to be true, at least so far. And today, as I was leafing through a long-forgotten 1970 journal, out fell a FIX HELLAS beer napkin, bringing with it the memory of two gorgeous French girls I'd met and hung out with in Herakleon, Mariedos and—I couldn't remember the other girl's name. Mariedos claimed to be something of a "voyante," and at our last dinner wrote my psychic analysis in ballpoint caps all over the napkin: *EQUILIBRE HARMONIQUE, SOCIABLE, ESPRIT ABSTRAIT, FANTAISIE, HUMOUR, INDEPENDANCE, NON-CONFORMISME, OPTIMISME.*

So where did I go wrong? I didn't *go* wrong. I've always been wrong, covering up the fact as best I can that I have spent my whole life feeling lonely and alone, as if, to use my grandmother's phrase, someone was walking on my grave. I keep some sort of balance, however, by regarding loneliness in perspective as useful rehearsal for the final loneliness of death.

The Physical

It's December. Covid or not, my year-end physical is at hand so, having passed my temperature check at the main door and been handed a new mask, I arrive at the third floor, enter an office and waiting room empty except for a few nurses masked to the eyeballs.

Now, when I go to the doctor I feel the obligation to entertain him or her, help them relax, as if I was an imposition, someone with something nasty they're forced to look at, touch or treat, something I have to apologize for, downplay my symptoms in order to make them feel better and their job easier. I feel I owe nurses the same consideration, but when one enters the office, before I can inquire about her health and family, she's preparing a needle to suck my blood and saying in a mask-muffled voice, "I'm baking a cake for Jesus." "Er, what?" I say. She repeats that she's baking a cake for Jesus. "I can't stand blood," I tell her. Then, "What kind of cake?" "Christmas, of course," she replies. Oh, Christ's birth, I muse to myself, eyes averted. Birth's an indignity for all concerned. It's disgusting. You'd have thought we'd have thought of a better way by now. It's an aberration, like me sitting here just about naked as a newborn, thin cloth covering my modesty. I close my eyes. "Over soon," she says. "Have you ever been to Jamaica?" *Think what you could do if you could fly.* I need to keep my blood-pressure low and fool the machine. Too late. I open my eyes and glance over to the machine with its numbers. Too high. I try to fly slow over gooseberry bushes, over red currents, above a haystack with my parents on top. "Open your eyes." A torch flashes into my eyes. I'm blind! It's off. I'm not blind. Somebody rolls in saying I have heartworm, but it's only the EKG machine to stick things on me, not in me. She leaves. Enter doc. Did I drink enough to pee? I ask myself. When do I pee? Where do I pee, and where do I leave it? I forget. "Have you ever had a heart attack?" "Not yet." *Forget the prostate, please. Not the prostate.* "There, you can get dressed now. Don't forget to get vaccinated." It may already be too late.

The Other Painting

Nursing home deaths are high. There's talk of Cuomo faking the numbers. I don't know, but pictures of elderly people waving through nursing home windows to relatives who cannot visit are very upsetting. They remind me of last fall when Eva, my mother-in-law, was spending her last days in assisted living, a time stressful enough even without Covid. I remember her staring out the fifth-story window across the car-loud Belt Parkway and the Harbor View Motor Inn to a line of sea. "Shall I push you closer? Do you want to go outside on the terrace? In the shade? In the sun? You like flowers." She shakes her head slowly. "I can see from here." These are her first words in weeks since she asked her daughter "Whatshisname?" pointing to me. I begin to babble. "Cookie? Candy? How was lunch? Do you want—?" "Don't bother," she whispers so low I can hardly hear. I look up at the overhead TV, picture on, sound off, quiz show. Her absent roommate's set is the same. I sit back down on the bed and wait for my wife to return from the business office. Eva's eyes fill. I look at the painting on the wall to her left, red-roofed boxy houses on a hillside rising to mountains you draw as a child, a curving bay, a balustrade with a huge urn full of something like blue hydrangeas, a lamppost above an operatic staircase going down to two small boats like pea-pod halves. Then I notice reflected in the glass another painting on the opposite wall, same town, different angle, the Mediterranean as someone who'd never left Coney Island might imagine it. "Do you like the paintings?" No response. I turn and am surprised to see she's crying, silently. I look down and see tiny thermals rising slowly off my fingertips and I can't stop watching until I decide to climb into the painting, which one doesn't matter. I grip the sides, heave myself up and in just as I hear a sob. I lean over the balustrade and look down at the bland sea. I want to see the boats rock in a swell, but they don't, still as stone. I want to see birds, feel a breeze. Nothing, hydrangea blossoms flat as numbers. I look around. Nobody. I see the other painting across the room with me reflected in it, ghostly. I would like to wave. I step out of the painting. "Would you like something to drink? Would you like to go down?" She is staring out the window. I look at the painting where nothing falls into disrepair, roofs look stuck on forever, the road that has never heard of potholes, shade that never moves, shadows that stay put. Suddenly, from behind, a yowl, unearthly, an animal in anguish. I spin round to a toothless mouth, open wide. "What, what, why—?" I manage. Silence. "Go down?" she whispers.

Brian Swann

Teeth

As I lie in the tub I feel I am hanging off the side of the world, weightless, or swaying on one of those cradles window-cleaners use to get at skyscrapers' glass. This is a small tub. This is a small bathroom suspended over a drop of ten stories, separated from eternity by a brick wall that can't be more than a foot thick. I take a deep breath, calm down, try to feel normal, reassure myself by washing my hair with what's left of a bar of Pears soap, chosen, not only because it floats, but because it made an appearance in *Ulysses*. Disgusting, my mother-in-law used to say, lying there bathing in your own filth. To escape her voice I get up, dripping all over the floor. Before I can dry off, my wife is at my side with comb and scissors. Since Covid prevented attendance at my regular barber, if you can call Astor Place Hairstylists "regular," she has kept what remains of my locks in some sort of order so I am less of a shaggy dog. Naked, I sit on the toilet lid and she snips away. After she leaves, I remember I hadn't cleaned my teeth that morning. I could have cleaned them in the tub, I suppose, but to what end? They have never been in great shape, even though as a child we lived just down the road from Dr. Billy Cowper, the family dentist who was also Curator of the Bagpipe Museum in Newcastle's Black Gate. He never used any painkiller when he drilled, and my screams must have been as ear-wrenching as those recorded bagpipes that were always playing when you entered his office, perhaps to drown out the screams. But as I grew older I came to love bagpipes, especially the Northumbrian small pipes, a passion I shared with Basil Bunting.[*] As I sat there on the toilet lid, deciding where and when to clean my teeth, wondering what state they were in

---
[*] For an account of my visit to the poet, see *St. Andrew's Review*, Spring–Summer 1977, as well as *Jargon* 66, 1977.

after so much neglect, pre- and post-Covid, I recalled a dentist I'd met years ago when I was looking for a house. Like Billy Cowper, he had two jobs. In addition to his dental practice, he also ran a real estate office. He'd driven me around in his beat-up Jag through a pretty depressing landscape, culminating in something being built on top of a hill surrounded by broken-down houses. "It's a restaurant," the dentist announced as we exited the Jag. "They're going to specialize in desserts. Not good for teeth, so good for business. You should think of buying in." Instead of thinking of buying in, however, I reconsidered my desire to move to this area. We drove around some more and were heading off into the sunset when he swerved violently to avoid the driver in front who had swerved to avoid a cyclist. "Women drivers," he hissed, before launching into an attack on driver education and the National Health Service, adducing as evidence the rotten state of English teeth.

The Other Side

Why are there so many newspaper clippings all over my desk, notebooks, address books, torn and creased maps? What's going on? What was I looking for? Did it have anything to do with a recent visit to pick up a shovel and plastic bags at the hardware store where the owner, Bruce, told me how he was looking for a security guard? He'd thought he had one, he said, until the guy turned out to be an ex-detective recently busted for stealing tires in places where he'd been sent to investigate the stealing of tires. No, it didn't seem to have anything to do with this. What was I looking for?

When I was a teenager I looked forward to a future in which I was a famous writer. To this end, I sent a short poem to the *Reader's Digest*, where my father had a subscription donated by a relative in Canada. My favorite section was "It Pays to Increase Your Word Power." This is the poem I sent: "The trouble with my camera / Is I come out like a chimera, / A fabulous beast / To say the least." They didn't respond, so I sent another about a rock, most of which I forget, but it ended with "So turn it over / To see what the other side reveals." Which brings me to a recent incident when I was driving along an empty highway in rocky Utah, or maybe South Dakota. No, Utah. Heat was rising in waves over the tarmac and though I was concentrating on the road ahead so as not to fall asleep, I still felt drowsy. Pinching myself, I decided to keep awake by alternating staring ahead with looking into the rear mirror until I found myself disappearing rearward, one-eyed and fabulous, but then something tickled my attention on the steering wheel. A fat white maggot was crawling over my fingers, in and out. I nearly crashed. Quickly, I pulled over onto the shoulder, stopped the engine, got out, opened the trunk, took out the shovel and a roll of plastic. I laid them down, opened all the car doors, pulled out and dumped all sorts of stuff, candy-wrappers, maps, socks, notebooks for an historical novel set in Virginia. Then I tore out the mats until I got to the one under the driver's seat. Slowly I lifted a corner, turned it over. A nest of squirming fat white maggots. I jumped back, stood as if transfixed, gradually becoming aware that a car had pulled up alongside with kids' faces pressed against the air-conditioned glass. I calmly shut all my car's four doors, then opened the driver's, got in and, waving, drove off into a horizon that seemed to recede all round. Whatever was under the floor mat would have to be taken care of later.

Yob

"Jesus is only a vegetation myth," I informed Mr. Barlow, my high school history teacher and verger at St. Botolph's.

"So what?" he said.

This stopped me in my tracks. I'd thought I'd had him.

I set *The Golden Bough* aside. What now? At fourteen, if you can't trust words, what then? But as I grew older I thought, who said you had to trust them? Maybe it's all a game, so I jumped on their backs and set off into a world not only of wandering vowels and impacted consonants but also where words didn't mean what they said, didn't mean what they looked like, that meant the opposite of what they appeared to say, that meant the same in one place and another in another, words that meant more than one thing or even nothing at all. Then one day I was reading an old copy of *transition*, the radically experimental magazine edited by Eugene Jolas that published many important modernists including James Joyce, Jolas' friend. I recalled how Aldous Huxley, who did not approve of this publication, expressed his opinion in print by writing the title backwards, more or less: NOITISNTART. Of course, I already knew of Llareggub and Erewhon, but it was from this encounter that my favorite words became those that economically and suggestively worked back to front, front to back, pushing and pulling like a shunting locomotive (there's a word for this, I believe). I first realized the serio/comic/cosmic implications when I lived in Rome and learned that Hadrian, that most literate of emperors, had on the Velia built the temple of Venus and Rome, fusing Venus, mother of Aeneas, the city's founder, with Roma Aeterna: ROMA AMOR. The temple's structure enacted its theme, each end echoing and replicating the other, an intense self-perpetuating architecture, a witty serious joke. It occurred to me that this phenomenon might even suggest a way to edit time, going forward, or backward, by going backward, or forward, even going forward in reverse. Or, more simply, it could be a story-source. For instance, a mad dam calls for imaginative exploration, as does a gnat with a tang, a god dog and a drab bard. This could go on and on into other worlds. In what circumstances would one pat a tap? Perhaps in a Chekhovian world where bookcases are apostrophized. And what kind of machine would emit time, what kind of world would exist with star rats? *Tar rat* might sound like something with Uncle Remus possibilities, while *sleek keels* suggests a Viking romance. *Slap pals* could be an S&M romance, and *lap pal* a friends-with-benefits soap. *Mood doom* evokes a piece based on *The Battle of Maldon* ("mod sceal the mare"), while *pool loop* contains compulsive aquatic possibilities and *garb brag* suggests a sartorial narcissism and *stab bats* possesses the possibility for the germ of a story of revenge visited on the source of the Covid virus. And so it goes on with possibilities rich and legion; yes, it's hard to stop with something "poetic" waiting in a wolf flow, something apocalyptic in *live evil* and *raw war*. As I went on, the world became more and more malleable, a world whose roots, I now realize, were not only in my questioning whatever I was presented with ("Is more interested in criticizing the French language than learning it," wrote Mr. Mantell in my end-of-term report), but also from the moment I came across *Peabody's Improbable History* in which I was Sherman the boy who played dog to Mr. Peabody whose very name suggested a vegetation god. I loved when Mr. Peabody looked at the camera and said, "Smart as a whip, ain't he?" From here my world expanded to the Wayback Machine of Shakespeare and King Arthur, especially when they scared Edgar Allen Poe so badly he had to write his scary stories, and even *Winnie-the-Pooh* and *The Wind in the Willows*. Ah, the shook-up infinite existence that made sense forward and back, up and down, even sideways, where a dog had a boy until it all came crashing down in a shower of grunts and snarls when the boy at 19 (me) became a yob in Teddy Boy clothes, velvet collar and winkle-pickers, smoking Craven A and Players on street corners, getting into fights. Who needed words when you had a cosh and knuckle-duster?

My Sister Eileen

Last night I was watching TV again, or what passes for TV these days of blur-out, fade-away and break-up, probably one of those Alaska programs, when I saw something that made me close my eyes and put my hands over my ears. A young woman was repeatedly stabbing a knife into an animal held below the camera's focus, twisting, turning, jabbing as if skinning it alive, a raccoon, maybe, a fox, rabbit, wolverine.… Next thing I knew I was running as best I could on crippled legs across a large field with a bull coming at me in the distance. I aimed for the high fence of logs, which I discovered had no way through except for cunningly designed gaps just wide enough for me to fit in but not through, and … And that was that, until this morning I woke to pins and needles in my feet and memories of my Uncle Len, my favorite uncle, my mother's sister's husband who spent his entire life working as a plumber in a Tyneside shipyard. During the war, when my father was away in the Navy, at the first whine of an air-raid siren, wherever he was, Uncle Len would run over to our house, leaving his wife to fend for herself, ignoring my mother and grandmother, grab me, dash into the garden and down into the air-raid shelter under the rockery. When years later we moved away, I stayed closer to him than my father. I remember a phone call toward the end of his life when I was about to start university. I asked, as usual, how he was keeping and expected the usual reply, "Canny, son." This time, however, I received a catalogue of all his aches and pains, in detail. It was what I usually got from Aunt Violet, but not him, and his reply embarrassed me. I didn't want to hear. This was not how he was, who he was, or who I wanted him to be. But as I lay in bed with my own aches and pains, from arthritic hip to gouty toe, I thought I understood, after all these years. I was not him. I was not even me. I stared directly above my head and for the first time in over thirty years noticed the wide beam stretching across the room exactly along my body. If it ever fell I'd be flattened. These buildings were erected after the war, sort of like me. For returning servicemen. How long does a building like this last? What is holding it all together still? How many people have lain down exactly where I lie now? The gale last night felt as if it could blow everything away. Originally this was marshland. If a hurricane stronger than Sandy struck, that would be it. If a quake hit—we are on fault lines—the land would turn to jelly and swallow us up. I rose and went to the window, looked down at moving vans lining the sidewalk taking people away, heard the whines and bleats of ambulances. Many years ago, I had been enticed to move to the city by the romantic movie *My Sister Eileen*. Like the heroine, I had a basement apartment. Mine was in 739 Washington Street, a West Village brownstone built in 1899 near the Hudson River that from time to time threatened to flow over the road and into my apartment. I was young. I loved and still remember its enchanted space, as I remember how in the movie the young woman looked up and out through her window at the magic passing by.

The Ladder

Though it was some time ago, I still recall how slippery and steep was the way there. In bottom gear, I barely moved forward, and the rain persisted. I narrowly avoided clipping a two-man road crew and was sure I'd be late, but when I finally arrived and parked the car the show had not yet begun. The crowd was peering down into the small empty amphitheater with vertical wooden walls that made me think of visits to the Spanish City at Cullercoats, source of a schoolboy joke: How do you get to Cullercoats? Answer: Dye them, (the name in fact means "dovecotes"). Yes, the Wall of Death, that was it, where a motorcyclist at the bottom revved up his machine to a roar and went straight up the wall, round and round, up and down. We waited for him to fall, since what he was doing didn't seem possible, defying gravity, and when another cyclist joined him going in the opposite direction I waited for them to crash into one another in an explosion of flame. The Wall of Death. I have never thought of death as a wall, nor as something to defy, like gravity, nor as a trick. How strange everything is, I thought, as I waited with the rest. How easy to be drawn into the impossible and see it as possible. As I looked down into the empty bowl, I remembered as a kid a man coming round our streets with his handcart. For a penny he'd let you look at a man from Borneo or Mars with a tail and feathers, the size of a small dog, or, for a penny more, a merman he kept under wraps with only a tail like a fish showing and a head like a monkey. Were they impossible? Not quite. I more than half believed, and remembered. I even think they were factors in my deciding to write my MA thesis on Sir Thomas Brown, particularly the chapter in his *Musaeum Clausum*, aka *Bibliotheca abscondita*, devoted to King Solomon's treatise on the shadow cast by our thoughts, somehow, as I recall, connected with Giordano Bruno's *De Umbris Idearum*. But to return to the show.

A man brought in a ladder and leaned it against the wall, where it reached to just below my nose. He was a histrionic gentleman whom I can best describe as Middle European, Hungarian maybe. The language he spoke into a bullhorn sounded unintelligible until, if you paid close attention you could make out English sentences well-constructed if difficult of accent which, strangely, lent authenticity to what he was imparting. He told us what he was going to do and then began to do it, climbing the ladder almost to the top, then reaching through the rungs and pushing the ladder away as if he was on a boat, shoving off from the bank. The ladder swayed a bit, wobbled, then stabilized. Perfectly balanced, he raised his arms in triumph. But this was only the beginning. He hopped, he skipped, he danced the ladder as if it was a limb. Could it be possible that I remember him bending the ladder in the middle, forward then backward, never losing balance? It was impossible to take your eyes off him. The audience was so rapt we forgot to applaud, even when the ladder stretched out almost horizontal and still he danced to an internal rhythm, never losing equilibrium.

Now, years later, it's true I'm not so sure of what I saw. Perhaps I was influenced by what I was reading at the time, probably Wittgenstein's *Tractatus* with its 526 numbered rungs we climb "to see the world right" and wonder at its existence. It's possible, but I do recall vividly when the impresario invited a child onto the ladder with him and then let the child, a boy of nine or ten, direct the proceedings, to the boy's great delight. Was he a plant in the audience? Does it matter? In my mind, the climax was even more improbable. Yes, I've read about shamans climbing into the rafters, throwing their voice, and then disappearing. But they were stories, anthropological at that. I've also seen a document on the Indian rope trick, but that was a cheat, though I don't know how it was done. This, I'm sure, was something else. We watched this child climb to the very top rung, raise both hands over his head, bend over, stand on his head, feet perfectly together. "Grab his feet!" the impresario instructed me from below where he was keeping the ladder steady. "Grab tight and no let go!" I did as instructed and then, I swear, I disappeared too, both of us, the child and me. Disappeared, or something close.

The Box

I looked about the roof-garden piled with junk and spare parts for machinery that kept the building working—the elevator going up and down, the air-conditioner cooling things off, the furnace warming them up. It began to occur to me that I might be at the wrong address, or I'd got the time wrong. How much time did I have? I walked among ailanthus growing luxuriantly, vines and lianas of all sorts, a rubber plant, all silent. Didn't Aristotle say plants live in perpetual sleep? Perhaps nobody was supposed to be up here, yet here I was, along with a rat or two and the hollow, sucked-out remnants of a small colorful bird, blue swallow-like tail, purple finch-like breast feathers, stuck in a small artificial tree. I tried to light my pipe, but it wouldn't work. I tried again, but the match blew out. *I will be important,* I said to myself. *I will light it.* I tried again, but the odds were against me. I sat on a log in the corner, then stood up again and found myself staring at a huge box lying on its side, like a sarcophagus, empty except for what looked like a squirrel's nest. Everything reminds me of something else, I said to myself, and this reminded me of the pine box my father had a carpenter friend make for me when I crossed the Atlantic for the first time in 1964.* It was constructed tight as the Ark with deep screws as if it was to make the journey by itself without aid of a ship. After the rough crossing, at the Cunard pier in Manhattan the customs man asked me how much it was worth not to open the box for inspection. I thought he was joking. He

---

* I crossed the Atlantic a few times. In September 1968, among the very few passengers on board the *United States* was the rock group Traffic en route to their first U.S. tour. Alone and bored in First Class, they spent the time getting drunk in our Tourist Class bar where the bartender hated them so much he tried, perhaps with some success, to poison them with increasingly bizarre drinks.

wasn't. I had $25 to my name. I told him. He walked away. I stood there until the pier was empty. He returned. How much do you have now? he asked. I told him. He walked away and returned with a huge screwdriver. When he'd done, my books were strewn all over, and it was dark outside. I spent an hour putting them back. I treasured that box. It stayed with me from apartment to apartment all over the eastern seaboard even after all the books had been lost, sold or discarded. I often draped an Indian print over it and on top placed a rubber plant or aspidistra. Finally, I left it in the attic of a Victorian house once owned by a famous Thomist. The box seemed safe there, empty under sturdy beams, stable on a wide-planked oak floor, safe from just about anything, and nobody any the wiser, reminding me that this Thomist wrote that man's substance is hidden from him. It is still there for all I know.

Jacques Maritain and the Shrew

Walking home yesterday, I saw a squirrel run down from a tree and begin tearing at a plastic bag filled with something. He made those little put-putting motions with his hands as when they bury a seed or nut and pat the soil down over it, hoping no one will notice where it's hidden. This time, however, I decided to look closer and I saw that, while someone had obeyed the law and picked up after his dog, he had then simply tossed the bagged poop aside, where the squirrel came upon it and was trying to find a way in as though it was a real treasure. Sensing a kindred spirit, I stood there and watched, my mind in neutral, until something rose from my brain like a carp from a pond, a quote from Doughty's *Arabia Deserta*, to the effect that while the ancient Semites had their foreheads touching heaven their feet were stuck in excrement. *Yes, I thought, I'm always slipping gears, always idling, but I do try hard to understand.* Often, however, I end up chasing my own tail. Yes, I try to get to the bottom of things but when I do there is only a trapdoor. Still, I attempt to join things, but since they fly off so easily, I try to tie them in, join them by their edges. I end with a fabric of edges. Who knows what's in between? Perhaps nothing. Dean Swift wanted to conduct an experiment "to write upon nothing." I suppose by "upon" he meant "on" or "about," but for me that word "nothing" also indicates the very topics I write on, and in the process feel myself immaterial. At the best of times, I have a hard time locating myself since I'm never quite sure where I am. As soon as I mark the spot, it takes off, sometimes me with it. So I change the subject, like now when I recall that Mozart copied down music he heard in his head, materializing the ideal. What a luxury, always spinning out. Body artists maim themselves, become self-consuming art objects. But I don't have their courage. Where am I? When I walk, the past is visible, sort of, in front, the rest is invisible, sort of, behind. In some cultures, the past is visible in front, the future invisible behind, which makes sense. Time flows in different directions in a number of ways, like motives. For instance, I was walking down the street the other day when I saw a man in an old gray suit carrying a pail of yogurt, reminding me of the yogurt-sellers I used to see in Kanlica, on the Bosphorus. I ran after him down the slight hill toward town, calling out that I needed yogurt, though I really didn't. He broke into a trot. When I caught up with him, "I'd like to buy your yogurt," I said. "It's already spoken for," he wheezed, out of breath. But then he said, "OK, I can spare this much," and he drew a none too clean finger across the creamy crust. "All the way to the bottom?" I asked. He looked puzzled. "How," I explained, "how can you translate your horizontal line into a vertical volume?" "OK," he huffed, "in that case and on second thought I need it all. I can't spare any. It's all or nothing." "All right," I said, "I'll take it all, though I don't know what I'll do with it." He looked offended again. "In that case," he said, "you can't have any," and continued on his way. I was remembering all this as I sat at my desk mid-morning thinking how George Eliot and other nineteenth-century novelists would have dealt with such a situation in their detailed, firm way of impressing themselves upon the world, phrasing and shaping it in language firm, sound and entire. Their worlds were solid as anything, even at a time when their world was wobbling, losing God, certainties and safe shapes. They even, as in *Middlemarch*, managed to construct a new mythos to replace the old, a myth as unironic as myth in *Ulysses* is ironic. As I was about to write down these thoughts, the phone rang. It was my accountant, Steve, asking me if I wanted him to file tax returns for my mother-in-law who had just died penniless, assisted living and nursing homes having eaten up all her savings, what she called her "legacy." I repeated his question to my wife. "Idiot," she muttered. "Of course not. Or what's the point in dying?" I conveyed the decision to Steve, hung up and returned to my desk. Yes, I was indeed an idler, living in shadows, even if the shadows were those I cast. Shadows, I thought, who was it said "I sell the shadow to support the substance?" All at once, out of nowhere, I felt my heart racing, playing havoc with its stents, beating as fast as a shrew's heart that, if you could hear it, would sound like a finger running through a comb. Since their metabolism is so high, if they can't eat while crossing a road they die. I ran to the kitchen, grabbed a hunk of cheddar, returned, and noticed a piece of yellowish paper at the back of my desk among bills under a bag of nuts. I pulled it out carefully and found, in my handwriting, a quote from Jacques Maritain, in whose study at 26 Linden Lane, Princeton, I used to live while writing my dissertation. When he died, Maritain left the large house to his dear friend, the "magic" (his word) composer Arthur Laurie, born Naum Izrailevich Luria, lover of Akhmatova, friend of Stravinsky. When Laurie in turn passed on, in return for my helping out about the place, his aged widow, Elizabeth, a Romanoff in exile, invited me to live in Maritain's study, still full of his books, papers, and letters. I remember many desperate epistolary calls for help and advice, soulful appeals from all sorts of people. One in particular stands out, from Henry Rago, editor of *Poetry*. But I digress. I unfolded the brittle sheet carefully and began to read about the soul searching for "a compensating victory, an illusionary eternity in the region of surfaces unfailingly arranged." I crumpled it up. What did "unfailingly arranged" mean if it all fails? What's the point? And as for eternity, it's just another form of the future which, as we saw above, is in the past. I didn't get the great Thomist then and I don't get him now. I don't get philosophy and I don't get theology. They miss so much, like economics. I sat back. My heart had slowed, but now floaters were crossing my eyes. I tried to follow them in their journeys as they wandered about. I tried to hold them in some shape, but couldn't. Perhaps, I thought, an algorithm could make sense of them, do for me what night skies did for our ancestors.

The Contortionist

They'll find there's less to me than meets the eye: these legs, for instance, bending like water and shoulders that slip in and out of sockets, integuments and tendons that torque and twist, spine so flexible I can roll like a hoop or whirl like a lariat until I vanish "before your very eyes," as they used to say if, of course, you can believe your eyes, because when you look there's nothing there, just the whiff of displaced air and people looking about asking "what was that?" before they wander off for the clean lines of the sword-swallower, flare of the fire-eater, bravado of the bearded lady or the man who strangles balloons into sausage dogs.

To a Head

For some time, I have been obsessed with disappearance. Do I want to disappear? I want to disappear. *Bite your tongue!* Which is what I have been doing, waking in pain at all hours of the night, tongue throbbing, mouth filled with blood, and the strong sensation that something is reaching up from the pit of my stomach, from deep in my gut to grab my tongue, drag it down, the rest of me following, turning myself inside out until I disappear, as if something long building is coming to a head.

Brian Swann

Modifying the Sahara

Yet, despite all this talk of disappearing, everything, including me, is alive. Nothing is ever lost. Energy is eternal, as the umpteenth law of thermodynamics states. This fact was brought home to me the day after I'd demoted my old and belled-out alarm clock to the other bedroom and, though I really had no need for a clock since my job was placed on hiatus, I went shopping online and found a new one with a youthful bell. But wouldn't you know it, I was wakened before dawn the very next day by a terrific noise: not the new clock, but the old one, which had found its youthful voice again, even if at the wrong time. Still, though it gave me hope, I needed to fill my sleep quota, so I lay back down, trusting in the new clock to call at the correct time. When it didn't, I dumped it and reinstated the old one, which was a mistake since it seldom worked again, and on those few occasions when it did function it reminded me of me: it ran to its own schedule and was not to be relied on. Its bell-tone was never the same twice, though it was always melodic, which was encouraging, since even in its sick dotage when time had lost meaning it still seemed to remember music, which brought to mind the saying that every sickness is a musical problem that requires a musical solution, yes, music, mimic of cosmic harmony, music of the spheres, the rhythm of desire, life's infinite pulse.... I was thinking these thoughts, though not in words, lying in bed looking at the cobwebs in the corners of my windows, where they had caught the odd piece of lint, dust, even a small insect, perhaps the very one who had made the web in the first place, which reminded me of the punchline of a fable, which one escaped me. In any case, these webs helped me think I lived more outside among nature than I actually did, in fact even relying on my laptop to go out into the world like Odin's ravens and come back with the news. This got me musing how I used to try to catch frost on the panes at the very moment when it started laying down the lines that grew into fantastic fractal cultures until, happening to turn my head, my eyes fell on the book that lay open under my mask on the bedside table. Soon I found myself reading about an Iroquois ceremony called an *ononharoin*, "turning the brain upside down," where dreams were acted out in charade, but you should only mime what you wanted most desperately; you could only riddle, not ask in words for the soul's secret desire. I began to think what I could mime, perhaps an atomic clock so I could resonate at the same frequency as the universe, then if somebody could guess my most inner desire I would go out and re-join the world, get back to my job, live a well-regulated life and do my bit for humanity, like the man who scooped up a handful of sand a few hundred feet from the Great Pyramid and let it fall a little further off in the desert saying *I am modifying the Sahara.*

Part Two: The Fourth Wall

Olive-O or Heptane

I left the hostel and climbed aboard a Circline tram empty except for a young woman and a girl who had just said something amusing. They both laughed, and I laughed too. The woman looked across the aisle. "Her name's Olive-O," she said, and we began a conversation, talking easily about this and that as the tram clattered along, a few people getting on, a few people getting off. Olive-O showed me her amber necklace and her cut-out paper dolls. I felt as if I had known them both a long time and would like to know them more, but "somebody's stolen my toothbrush," I said, and got off at the next stop.

    I had no idea where I was as I stood in front of what looked like a looming amphitheater. I walked in through the *Exit/Entrance* gate and found myself standing on white dust surrounded by what looked like white cliffs; I was in a blazing white bowl. Looking about, squinting, I felt I had been tricked into seeing something there was no need to see, until I noticed a large woman in a handmade tunic of what looked like hide, reindeer, deer, her thick gray hair down to her waist, bare feet. She was speaking to someone I couldn't see in the shadows, her words coming over as barely more than clipped syllables, the way I imagine Neanderthals might have spoken. She turned, retrieved an antler pick like those I'd seen at the flint mines of Grime's Graves, and went over to hack at the chalk wall at eye-level, enlarging a small cave. Chunks fell off as she muttered to herself. *An experimental archeologist?* I thought. No one to ask, I decided she was the custodian of or guide to this silent, flat caldera, cliffs like Dover, honeycombed like the sea-rocks at Naxos, bright as the falls at Pamukkale, barren except for a couple of hollow trees. I saw a young man and walked over. "How old is this place? I inquired. "Very old," he replied. I walked over to the larger of the trees and kicked it as if an echo could give me a clue, like ground radar. "But what's time got to do with it?" the young man added. "True," I said. "There was a time when time was disallowed as not very helpful. It got in the way." He nodded. "Well, I continued, "what is this place?" He waved a hand around. "The quarry for the new city," he said. "The new, not the old. Or maybe it was the other way round. In any case, after the plague." I wrote this down in my notebook.

I'd almost completed the circuit when a flash of light caught the corner of my right eye. A jewel-like drop of resin was hanging from a gash in a branch. Heptane, I said to myself, is distilled from resin and used to measure petrol's resistance to exploding under pressure. Gingerly I reached out. Not sticky. Odorless. Colorless. This made me angry, as if I had been fooled. I kept a notebook in my pocket for such an occasion. I took it out, looked, pulled off the remaining page, which I tore to shreds and tossed into airless air. As I wandered round, seeing what there was to see, I found myself just outside the Entrance/Exit. There was the woman from the tram, with Olive-O. She was talking to the reindeer-woman. I sidled up closer, concealing as much of myself as I could behind scraggly bushes but I couldn't make out what they said. I crept closer. The woman was talking about her husband, how she's left him, how he was so negative about everything, always complaining about being lonely, depressed, seeing no good in anyone, trusting no one, prone to outbursts followed by abject apologies, always expecting the worst, unable to connect with anyone, even Olive-O. Flattening myself against a wall, I reached for my notebook but couldn't find it. I slipped by without being noticed, walking down the cypress-lined lane until something made me stop and turn.

There was Olive-O waving a scrap of paper in one hand and a cut-out paper doll in the other. I almost wanted to wave back but was distracted by a large drop of resin in a cypress tree caught by the sun.

Brian Swann

History

The house I've just sold is huge and wonderful. I can't imagine why anyone would want to sell it. I outline again for the two buyers its special features: two fireplaces down and two up, all working. I had no occasion to say this, but they reminded me of the poet John Patrick Creagh's old Chianti farmhouse in Radda, which, though it only had one fireplace, was big enough for him, his wife Ursula and their children to sit in, big enough to roast an ox in, and in fact we did roast a pig in it once. "There used to be three fireplaces more upstairs," I tell them before moving on to list and describe the comfortable furniture, distinguished paintings, fine décor and so on, most of which was true. I like to be upfront. "Worth every penny you paid," I say. "Even more. Let's go outside." I really don't want to go outside, but we do. Here I show them the venerable barn with huge oak beams. Tack hangs from the walls, horse collars. There are stalls with no horses, reins and bridles here and there, wheels and axles, even an old milk-float with broken shafts. I leave them to it, walk off to the car, get in, not really paying attention. Why would anyone want to sell? I drive off. Soon I'm lost. I thought I knew that area, but clearly I don't. Careless. I turn onto a side road from the side road I'm on and stop for gas at one of the two gas stations across the road from each other. I like the way the Getty sign sways invitingly. But no gas comes from the pump. "We're out," he says. I look across the road. "Him too." I ask for directions. "Go back the way you came," he says. "Then take a left." I don't want to go back the way I came so I cross the road, locate a lady attendant, and fill up. I ask her the same question and she gives me exactly the opposite direction. "Keep going up the hill to the right," she says, "the way you were going. Then take another right.

That'll take you where you want to go." How does she know where that is? I decide to take the first advice, turn round and eventually find myself back at the house I'd sold. Parking the car in the driveway, I go inside. Three workmen push by me and run up the stairs. They start to hammer. I follow. "Hey," I call out, "what are you doing? This place is mine." They ignore me, joking among themselves. Then one looks up. "We've already been paid to do this work," he says, and goes back to screwing something into something else. Outraged, I run downstairs, grab the wall phone and call the police. It takes some time, but when I finally get through and explain the situation, the voice at the other end tells me there's nothing she can do. So I decide to take matters into my own hands, dash up to the main bedroom and, rummaging under the bed, feel for the baseball bat. Waving it about, I return to the workmen, hoping they'd get the hint and I wouldn't have to belabor the facts. But again they ignore me until someone I take to be the foreman arrives. "Look," he says, "we're only doing this part here, that's all. We were paid by the previous owner." "That was *me!*" I shouted. "In that case," the man says, "what's the problem?" and walks off. Good question, I think, looking out the floor-to-ceiling window to what appears to be a picnic or jamboree on the lawn. I am of two minds to join them, but don't. You can pick up things from crowds, pathogens, viruses. I go downstairs as people are piling in the front door. A woman in a floral hat pushes by me and into the kitchen where she pours herself a cup of coffee, takes a sip then, with an expression of disgust, pours it down the sink. Who are these people? I am reminded of JP telling me how one evening he returned from a hard day in his vineyard to find hunters in his kitchen gathered around the massive wooden table, criticizing his Chianti as they drank it, criticizing his prosciutto as they cut slices from the haunch hanging from the beam over their heads. "Say anything," JP had told me, "and they burn down your house. In their minds, all this still belongs to them. Always will. History never happened."

The Conqueror

I felt I would have missed the train, bus, plane, whatever would have taken me there, but in the event I found myself where I wanted to be without much trouble. And when I arrived I dropped my stuff off and took a stroll along the ha-ha, careful not to tumble down. Ha-ha! There was no one about so I returned to my room for a nap, only to find my four-poster occupied by four sleeping youths who, no matter how politely and forcefully I requested their departure, would not wake, let alone move, even when I pulled the bedclothes off them and tried to shove them out the door. They just pushed back, got into bed and pulled the sheet over their heads. Mm. I took out my wallet. "Somebody's stolen my money!" I cried. "I left a mark to let me know if my wallet had been disturbed and not only has it been disturbed but my money's gone!" Still no response. Still they slept. So I left to inform the authorities, only to be nearly trampled by a crowd rushing up the staircase. People were everywhere, complaining there were people everywhere, protesting that all the food in the kitchen was gone, dashing here and there trying to get into rooms already full. And just where, I thought, was the host? When I asked anyone, no one knew. Why had he invited so many people? Was this to be another *Decameron*? In fact, I didn't know the man that well. A short time before, I'd happened to bump into him on Hyde Park Corner where we were both listening to a large man from the Caribbean arguing that disease was punishment for sin while next to him a gentleman from the League of Empire Loyalists was arguing that since the ancient Egyptians had no word for "art" or "religion" they had no art or religion and hence no culture. We walked across London, exchanging stories of people we'd known. He told me that his lineage went back to the Conqueror. I'd cracked a joke whose punch line was "Norman Mailer," but he didn't get it. Maybe his line did go back to William, who cares? I had no way of knowing. My lineage went back to shipyards and coalmines. Who came out better? And where was he now? Why were we all here? What did he have in mind?

The Matter

I just can't let go of the house we sold a few years ago. Now and then I sneak back in when no one's there and live as if nothing has happened, nothing has changed. I'm very careful. When I cook I don't use too much gas and before I leave I roll back the meter a bit, just a bit, just in case. Anything whose place I've altered I move back to its original location. I keep a chart. When I drink wine or liquor I make up the difference in water as I did when a kid at my father's liquor cabinet, which made him complain about the decline of manufacturing quality. Yes, I live frugally and carefully, which is no sacrifice. I am careful and frugal by nature. On my visits, things generally go well, no reports of home invasion, no neighbor complaints. I might even say I leave things better than I find them. For instance, if there are any spills on kitchen counters or on the floor I mop them up with rags I bring and take back with me. I make a point of making the bed so it looks as though nobody at any time had slept there. I puff up the pillows, smooth the coverlet. Yes, I do a very good job so even the police give me a friendly wave as I leave, and I wave back. But last night was different. So far, as I said, things had gone well. But last night was different. When I got there, I found the house full of strangers, rather coarse people, what my mother would have called "common." Luckily, there were so many it was easy to mingle and get lost among them until someone, without provocation, attacked. I was so badly beaten that one of the crowd, perhaps with good intentions, tried to stick something like an IV tube into my arm. Luckily, I recognized it as a live witch-duct inverse prophylactic and quickly pulled it out. Scrambling to my feet, I gave as good as I got, lashing out indiscriminately since there was no way to discriminate. I kicked, punched, bit before effecting my exit, rather the worse for wear. This, I knew, would be the end of things as they were. Someone had squealed. Someone had pulled the plug. I had little say in the matter. I had to let go.

The Morgan

John at the front desk has his Bible open. He is deep in discussion with a sceptic. "Have you ever seen the Pacific?" he asks. "No," says the middle-aged man in gym clothes. "Do you believe it exists?" "Well, yes." "There you are then," says John, patting the book and beginning to process a new membership for a woman waiting patiently off to the side.

To get to the changing rooms I pass the chlorinated pool and climb the stairs. I open a locker and start to undress. Music floats up. I turn to the large naked black man next to me. "What's that?" I ask. "Platters," he says. "No, I mean where's it coming from?" "I tol' you, the Platters." A larger naked black man joins in. "Maybe it's the lifeguards." "The lifeguards? Ain't never heard tell of *them*." "The pool." "They was great with Alex Hodge," says the first man. "Oh, sure," I say, joining in, faking it, "What was the other guy…?" "Alex Hodge," says the second man. "Paul Robi replaced him."

After the gym I take the bus uptown to check on Darryl's MG. It's fine, so I climb to the third floor to tell him my Platters story. "Yea," he says, "great group. I love 'Earth Angel.'" "Really?" I say, "I'm pretty sure that's not them. That was—." But he is already off to prove his point, scrambling about in CDs, iPhones, LPs and 45s. He is about to boot up Google when "OK," I say. "You're right. Maybe." But that isn't enough. "I'm definitely sticking to my guns," he says. I look out the window, down to the street. "Back in a minute," I say. People are sitting on his red MG, smoking. They've stolen bits of it in the past and will again if I don't move them off. There's a kid with an Afro like a halo in the driver's seat. "Out," say. He tells me to perform impossible anatomical feats on myself, but eventually climbs out. I go back upstairs where Darryl is hovering over drawings and blueprints for gloves that strengthen your hands and others that strengthen your feet. He says he has a backer for this, but not yet for another project which is to create pants with special copper bands and fibers that strengthen the glutes and abductor muscles all at the same time without any effort on the wearer's part. He lost me when he described something that seemed based on an egg carton worn when and where the need arose. He has lots of ideas. He himself is an amazing physical specimen, even in late middle age. He's always working out lifting weights, stepping, like now, up and down on a stool, doing push-ups with a clicker in one hand. As a means of subsidizing his inventions, he works as a special trainer to a number of celebrities whose names he mentions in a hushed voice as if it was a secret. His charisma and success derive, he says, from the fact that he was the only black man on the U.S. Olympic bobsled team. He looks up from a drawing.

"Why did you rush down. What's happenin', man?"

I tell him,

"Impossible," he says. "I'm a well-respected member of the East Harlem community."

"I know you are. But they still try to steal from you."

"What's missing?"

Here I'm stuck because I always try to arrive before anyone has had a chance to lift anything. Not always. But mostly they seem to have other things to do at night.

"Nothing," I say.

"There you are. Nobody. Nothin'. They wouldn't do that. I'm their bro. They're my homies. They respect me."

"Well, they don't respect me," I say. "You've turned me into a house ni—into a cop."

"You've turned yourself. Chill. And as you may have noticed, there's nothing in that car to steal. That's why I leave the top down."

"They steal bits. They fill it with garbage."

"Then where is it?"

"I pick it out and dispose of it before you can get down and see it."

"There you are. Whenever I use the car it's clean as a whistle."

"Exactly. Why do you leave it on the street anyway? There's a garage down the block."

"Nobody bothers me. Why do you keep asking? Feeling guilty?"

"For what? Got anything to drink?"

I knew he hadn't. He was a teetotaling, non-smoking vegan. He put some papers in a box.

"I'm going to Pakistan next week. Sign up some good cheap sewers. Can you keep an eye on the car?"

"You know," I protested, "I have a life of my own."

"No you don't, and yes, as you say, nothing will happen but I might put the cover on, just in case."

He dropped to the floor and did fifty pushups. Then stood up, not even breathing heavily.

"Before that MG down there I had a Morgan."

"A horse?"

"I'll bring you something back. Do you like chiapattis?"

"They're Indian."

"OK, but do you like them?'

"How about paying what you owe, reparations? Why don't you sell the car? It's in good condition. You seldom drive it."

"Maybe when I get back. Wanna make an offer? I'm looking at a Ferrari GTC 4 Lusso."

"Dream on, bro. But, as you always say, this is America. Gotta go."

I turn to leave, then turn back.

"What's a morgan?"

That's Life

I was talking with him again last night, this time in an apartment he'd sublet and whose poet-owner would later sue him for wrecking. "'Beau Geste,'" I said, apropos of nothing. "Your name reminds me of. Mine's a pig-herder." "Pigs don't herd," he said. "Right," I continued, "but, but it reminds me—." "Wasn't that a 1939 movie with Gary Cooper?" He took a puff at his Schimmelpenninck Duet, the kind that will kill him. "I think so," I said. "Susan Haywood. I loved her." "The dead were propped up on the parapet," he mused, stirring a liquid so black the spoon could hardly move. He called it 'mother-in-law tea.' "Yes," he continued. "The Foreign Legion. From a P. C. Wren novel." He saw me neglecting my tea. "Perhaps you'd like some more whiskey with that," he said, pointing over to a case of Jameson Irish Whiskey in the corner. "An admirer sent me." I shook my head, deciding any addition would make the tea even worse. "It's good," I said. "Just letting it cool." Then "Oh, I need a spoon." I got up and walked over into the kitchen. Stuff all over, but no spoon. Out of curiosity, I pulled the handle of the dishwasher. Out poured a Niagara of roaches. They ran, crawled, scattered all over the floor, all over my feet. I stomped, hopped, shook my legs until he rushed in. "Hey!" he called out. "Stop! What are you doing?" "Roaches," I panted. "All over!" "Stop it!" he said. "That's life."

Back in the living-room, talk turned to the historical novel, one of which I was thinking of planning out with a plot based on *The Raw and the Cooked*. "Done that," he said. I must have forgotten. He went on to outline his method which had no need for a lot of research. "Just stick in a few colorful facts and phrases," he said, "from time to time." I was about to argue for plentiful, even redundant research, when I remembered him coming downstairs. "Who wrote *Paul et Virginie?*" he asked his wife. "Abbé Prevost," she told him and he dashed back upstairs. "He's writing the article on The Novel for the *Encyclopedia Britannica*," she explained. "Doing it all from memory. He hates libraries and won't use them because he'll get too much material." And on we talked, into the wee hours: Joyce, Shakespeare, L. C. Knights, music, taxes, Belli, Moss Lane, Stephen Daedalus, Stephen Foster—Stephen Foster? I loved him, reason enough. And on and on. He particularly liked when I informed him that his was the same as the English name of Wovoka, The Paiute Prophet, founder of the Ghost Dance Religion. That evening he told me many new stories, my favorite being the one about his father playing the cinema organ for silent movies. One performance he fell asleep. When he woke, he looked up from the organ pit and saw a party going on, so he played "For He's a Jolly Good Fellow." It was *The Last Supper*. He was fired. It was very late when I let the subway take me back downtown. I got off at the wrong stop,

Next morning, over a glass of Alka-Seltzer, I tried to recall the events of the evening before, starting with roaches, at a distance admiring their ability to survive even atomic attack. Soon I found myself contemplating their cousin, the virus, whose purpose, I decided, was to be itself as fully as possible, even if that meant constant change in response to circumstances; being so in love with its function of taking on the world that it disappeared into itself and so triumphed. Without a bone in its body it knows exactly what it's doing, so I decided that the more bones you have the more confusion. Ah, to be a single gene infinitely replicated, the absolute life form that lives through death. Is the virus conscious? Does it have a subjective experience of life, a felt quality? What was in that tea? What was in that whiskey? A raw egg might do it. Tylenol? It can be shut down but not out, the virus. There will always be one somewhere. There are more viruses than numbers. That's life. If I feel better by lunch, I say to myself, I'll take her out, but not to the place we went to yesterday, one of those Village places with steep steps you're in danger of tumbling down. She had insisted on saying hello to the owner who she said she knew. But he wasn't there. A waiter came over to our table and asked if we were ready to order. She was already put out and said nothing. I asked for what somebody like me would order in a restaurant like this. She asked for vodka. After a while, the waiter returned with empty hands. Sorry, he said, but I couldn't find the vodka. That's life, I said. I had to go to the bathroom.

Old Friends

I wake at dawn, stomach in knots, as usual, afraid, this ancient Anglo-Saxon *uhtcearu*, dawn-sorrow, the mind *put-put-put*ting, an old two-stroke pushing uphill, going nowhere, "a stagger in air," until words skitter, crowd in, *crowd*, a Welsh harp, twang, twang, the bird outside the window never stops, thinks the city's lit forever, never going out, one note repeated, quoting itself, pinging like radar, fooled by light the way the park itself is fooled, twisted to our will with flower-beds and footpaths, and here I am each day waking to a man practicing the same scale up and down and that deluded bird's one note as if that's all he's got while I lie among dead and missing friends, beyond the pandemic, long ago and far away, as close as my old friend Seamus there cross-legged on the living-room floor like an old Cheyenne story-teller, smoothing the ground, "we men of the north," he inscribes on the fly-leaf as he talk bog burials and oaks flattened by gales from the east, still dug up from East-Anglian fens the Dutchmen drained, wood now valued for its grain, carved and shaped. "The end of art is peace," he says, getting to his feet. "Magari," I say, staying where I am.

These Things Being So

Clothes piled everywhere, mostly men's. Hardly a peg was free, but I found one near the door and hung from it my new velvet underpants. The rest of my clothes I piled in a corner where I knew I could easily retrieve them. I pulled on the bathing suit I'd been handed, but it didn't really fit. It reminded me of the thin green string thongs Dr. Sherman distributed at the green pool our school used to use. They barely covered our not-yet adolescent private parts and certainly did not cover those of Lewis Stone who was our age but way ahead of us developmentally. He was hairy and had a bird's nest down there. Dr. Sharman who taught Latin and ran the Crusader's Bible group we belonged to, patrolled the steamy chlorinated pool edge, hooded eyes lowered, tweed jacket buttoned, tie knotted. I used to see him in town riding his big green Raleigh bike, reminding me of Boadicea on a Clydesdale. Years later, I read in the paper that he'd been arrested. Anyway, *quae cum ita sint*, or, these things being so, back to me again, years later, walking over to the green pool and diving in, a good clean dive. When I broke the surface and looked around, expecting some sort of appreciation for my dive, if not applause, all I got was a comment from my friend Justin: "You bent your legs." For the first time, I realized he looked like Lewis Stone. I began a breaststroke. *This isn't as much fun as I hoped*, I thought. Why was I remembering these people? Was something bad going to happen and I needed to remember everything before it was too late? I turned onto my back, doing a dead-man's float, the only stroke, if stroke it could be called, that my father, an old Navy man, ever taught me. He said it would be useful for all occasions. As I stared up at the ceiling, there were Lewis Stone and me walking side by side across the school playing field when, with a gasp and a thud he fell forward, a javelin sticking out of his back. I turned over and began a vigorous crawl and, after a few strokes, began to enjoy myself until I noticed I was swimming through clumps of what felt like feathery algae. Pushing them aside, I climbed out of the pool and was about to go back down the stairs to the changing room when I noticed near the children's pool Jerzy arriving with Kiki, his girlfriend. She was a striking figure; "statuesque," I believe, is the word. Jerzy, on the other hand, was hollow-chested, thin and small. They reminded me of those figurines from Crete and Mesopotamia of a large Mother Goddess with, by her side or on her lap, her much smaller son/consort. In any case, Kiki saw me, waved, and did a lovely swan dive into the deep end, sending water and algae flying. Behind her, Jerzy tiptoed to the kiddies' pool and sat on the edge. I made my way down the steps toward the changing room but half-way to the bottom I had to pass Justin sitting at a table on the landing with his pals. They were chugging beer and eating sandwiches. "Join us," he said and, shivering, I did, briefly, but, "See you in a bit," I said, getting up. "We'll still be here," said Justin. I continued on to the changing room where clothes were piled every which way, all over, on top, everywhere, even to the ceiling. Each peg had a dozen items hanging from it. My peg was dangling from its fastenings. *How will anybody ever find anything?* I thought. *How will I find mine? I can't go out as I am and I can't just put on whatever comes to hand.* I picked up a bra and panties and put them back. How did they get there? Glancing about, mentally I tried on this, I tried on that, and then I picked up the courage to really try items on. Other men were doing the same, some leaving seemingly satisfied, others grumbling. Some were just chucking stuff around. Feeling a bit like a caddis fly, I found Justin and his crew where I'd left them. "Join us," he said again. I couldn't think of an excuse not to, so I did. He handed me a beer. "Those clothes don't fit," said someone. "What do you expect?" I replied. "Giant clothes upon a dwarfish thief." I looked about. "You look rather nice," said Justin. "Much nicer than this lot." He waved a wide arc. For a while, I sat with them as they bantered, wondering if this was all déjà vu, if, for instance, Jerzy had already told me how he managed to avoid the fate of Sharon Tate at the hands of the Manson gang, or he was about to tell me. Was he about to jump out from behind a sofa at a party, as he often did to scare people, or had he already done so? Perhaps both. Or—I decided that whatever was the case, next time I went swimming I wouldn't use the changing room. I'd go fully prepared. Or I wouldn't go at all. I'd stay where I was, as I was, wherever that might be.

Old Clothes

I've always been a floater. The only thing holding me together as "me" is the memory of someone inside the someone I "am" who makes choices unknown to me. I think it was William James who said consciousness is "the alternation of flight and perchings." I wish it was that concrete. He called for a "reinstatement of the vague and inarticulate to its proper place in our mental life." But that is far too articulate for my state of being. I was thinking this when I arrived at the cottage, parked the car, opened the front door. "Hello, hello, anybody home?" I called. I walked from room to room. "Hello, hello." One call would have sufficed for the whole house, since the rooms were hardly larger than a closet. Also, I assumed nobody was home, which was the reason I decided to spend time there. I walked into the living room. "Welcome, welcome!" he said warmly, which was surprising, since I hardly recognized him. "How are you?" said a lady, presumably his wife. "How are you?" "Here," said the man, "give me a hand with these, would you? We're cleaning up. Much too much stuff here. We're dumping it outside." "Oh, sure," I said, "but I can't find my shoes and it's raining." "No, it's not," he said, "and what you're wearing's fine." "And here," said his wife, pushing a pile of old clothes into my arms, "follow me. I'm making a heap at the end of the garden. Some might fit you." I had no choice in the matter. Circumstances denote necessities and vice versa. I followed them down the flagstone path. Not knowing if I was flying or perching, I did as I was told. Writ in water.

Personal

A floater, floating... I was lying in bed, half-listening to ambulance banshee wails, half-listening to small sound-waves rolling in, half-thinking about the Zoom course yesterday, The Personal Essay, where again I advised students to be "honest" and "authentic," wondering why they don't ask if I've ever written one and how if they do I'd say my mind doesn't work that way and how they'd look puzzled and say How come then you teach this course? and I could say I teach what I cannot do, and I think about masks, personae, how persons and the personal are personae, how things change from moment to moment and we do too so we're just memories linked and unlinked, reliable and unreliable, verifiable and invented (*The Invention of Tradition* is one of my favorite books), who knows? Fractured selves composed of our own and others' bits watching and commenting each on each, and the present is just the most recent past, the "authentic" and "honest," what feels right even with little or no proof, so we take the Kierkegaardian leap of—I turn on my side, look past the pot of small succulents to a blank sky with one tubby cloud doing things that remind me of Benny Hill, or the Benny Hill music, and I drift to Rhona Newton John, my friend from the Morley Memorial Primary School in Cambridge, she who scared the boys by looking up our shorts and making fun of us, she who ended up connected with the Profumo scandal and who when asked her profession by the judge said "Whore, m'lud," and who was a model and actress who appeared on *The Benny Hill Show*, ending up in Hollywood with her sister Olivia who I remembered as a baby in a pram wheeled by her German mother Irene on Hills Road outside the Cambridgeshire High School for Boys (the "County") where her husband, the Welsh baritone Brin

Newton John, was my headmaster at a school hated by Martin Amis and Roger Waters, whose mother was my teacher at the Morley and who featured the place in *The Wall*, and where most of Pink Floyd went including Roger Barrett who took my uncle Syd Barrett's name because he admired his jazz band, and who later lived with his mother next door to my sister and blocked the drains with sanitary napkins and brought the fire brigade frequently to put out the fires in the garden where he burned his paintings, and—. I got up, carefully, so as not to disturb Roberta. The succulents looked very precise, as if etched, and there I was in the window having dinner in '60s Princeton at my friend Al de Grazia's with Peter Tompkins and Tom Kuhn. Al, distinguished NYU social scientist and champion of Immanuel Velikovsky, he of *Worlds in Collision*, was refereeing a heated debate between Tom, he of *The Structure of Scientific Revolutions*, and Tompkins, he of *The Secret Life of Plants*. Science and non-science. I have always found myself wandering between and among them, floating in wonders.

Living Lightly with Kierkegaard

My wife was preparing breakfast as usual, but today felt different. As I looked about, I realized we were in the house we'd sold recently to a large Indian family named Pandya. What if they returned, I thought, if only for the day? I mentioned this to my wife. "Yes," she said, emptying out some water into the sink from the kettle she'd just set on the stove to boil. "You're right. They'd know. Or they'd be able to tell from whatever we use. We'll have to use less." She poured out a bit more water, measuring carefully. "This way they won't know. They'd have no way of measuring." For a moment I felt reassured, but then, "What if they do turn up?" I said. "What do we say?" She turned to me. "On a day like this?" I looked out the window at dreary fields. "You never know," I replied. "And I resent being made to feel like revenants." I sat down at the table and thought about the matter. I couldn't, for example, see them dashing down to the basement and measuring that little nipple oil-gauge thingy on top of the tank. They'd have to have been suspicious first and they'd also have had to know how much oil was in to start with. "We'll have to live lightly," I declared as I watched a Scotch mist descend over the valley, "light on the land, leave no traces." "Ecological," my wife added, "responsible." I turned back from the window and noticed how empty the house was, emptier than when we'd sold it, and we'd sold it furnished. I was startled back by a distant clatter of thunder like plates falling (we'd left them plates too). A strobe of lightning bounced off the one remaining mirror and fractured on the blank ceiling like the northern lights, "or like the revealed ache in a sheet of glass," I said to myself, relishing the image. "Light giving up its nerve, the little ..." My wife's voice brought me back. "Yes," I said, not sure what she'd said but risking a yes. "Good," she said. A fly buzzed. I looked up to where the ceiling stretched up high, rafters straining to keep it all together, like stitches. By rights, the walls should have bulged outward like a herniated disc. What the house needed, I decided, was a pillar or two. A pillar is the most appealing part of any house that is more than just a place. It lends distinction, as well as stability. I remembered reading how a pillar was the most frequent attribute of a Minoan sanctuary, at Koumasa, for instance, or at Knossos with its limestone pillar room, each rectangular pillar carved from a single limestone slab (sometimes it was carved from gypsum), or how the four painted pillars in a Pawnee earth-lodge supported and maintained the cosmos.... Yes, we may have made a mistake selling the house, though there was always a lot of work to do to keep it habitable, this house made entirely of wood so in storms it creaked like an old sailing ship on the ocean. You could almost hear the songs of mermaids amplified like whale song. It sat on a rock ledge over wetlands and could have fallen in. The wetlands (we used to call them swamps) lay like a flat green handkerchief. They—all at once it occurred to me that we should never have owned a house in the first place since I never felt I *could* own one, any more than I could own the swamp, or the ocean for that matter. Owning means being connected to something in an unequal relationship and I couldn't decide on which side of the equation I lay. Besides, there is always more and more that you are responsible for, and being so tied down means loss of freedom. After a while you lose the sense of perspective and start to see reflections of yourself everywhere, everything you see you own, the burden of egotism. So why this house? Why this, why that? It's because you've split yourself and there are lots of you everywhere. Nothing is fresh. You are what Kierkegaard called "the vast penitentiary" built of the reflection in you of everything you associate with. There is no house. It's all a big scam, and you the scammer. I looked up from these thoughts to see my wife looking at me curiously. "I'm thinking we ought to leave now while the going's good," she said. I was beginning to think Kierkegaard should be able to provide a way out of our dilemma, but I didn't want to enslave myself to any way of thought and sat down to breakfast.

Work

I was following an old deer track in the back field when a line of cows appeared on the horizon. *Why don't we breed them with deer?* I thought. Then I remembered that we had. We call them Jerseys. Off to my right a group of women was heading in the direction of town. When I bought this place it was virtual wilderness after the collapse of the dairy industry. The locals resented me, so who were they to walk on it now after my improvements? I yelled to them to clear off or I'd have them arrested. "Good luck with that," called out a large woman wearing a red bandanna. Suddenly I lost belief in what I was doing. The feeling of worth fell away. Years ago, just before he died my father told me what a great disappointment I was, no big house to visit. Now I had one, where was he? The trail petered out. Mists rolled in. I returned to the house, crossing the dry stream bed beside the ditch into which water was flowing from under the back door. It all still needed work. It was pointless to ask why. Why?

The Window

Halfway through the night, a moan, a groan, a scream. It won't stop. I can't place it, male, female, child, adult, below, across the way. Then it stops until dawn when I am wakened again and consider calling the police. But what can I tell them? I had, after all, gone to bed after reading "The Murders in the Rue Morgue" again. Perhaps it is nothing. Perhaps it is all in my head. I close my eyes and drift back to where I am a boat on the river, an old farmhouse on the mountainside, a tall pine, the smell of burning fields, farmers lighting wheat stubble after harvest, smoke drifting everywhere at once aromatic and stifling then, deeper, I am on my way somewhere I don't want to go, leaving the same place but never arriving, and I cough, consumptive, where *somehow a stubble plain looks warm* though air quality is poor because of the eruption of the volcano Tambura, and I open my eyes on a train heading north to my childhood home, a place I don't know and never want to visit, telling myself I'll never go back to that, yes, open your eyes and look into the window for the world but a face stares back weeping silent slow tears, single, then a full flow rolling down the cheeks, mouth open in a moan, a scream, as if trying to say something it doesn't want anyone to know, something it may not mean, but means, twisting to anger, faking to smile, then anger at its anger, its pain wrapped up tight in itself and so able to know nothing, not even its own anger, its pain. The face has melted into the glass, glass and no glass. There is no point, no point to start from, but there are appearances to keep up, lies to uphold, a life to make and make up.

Insect

Black-eyed Susans, tansy, pansy, scarlet flowers of the scarlet runners and now the new moon that sits and rocks under the evening star just over the pines and my deck with a few wind-blown maple leaves, crimson and black smudges, brown with a bit of white even though it's only August, leaving like words lovely for a while with desire or regret or something else while people die of Covid, misrule, and the rest. I go upstairs, but as I write I think of these fallen, shattered families, the president debasing truth and words, and I feel worse than foolish writing this, especially when so easily distracted by a fly, size of this "i" or less, who's slipped through the screen designed to keep him out, who begins to pop about, thrip-like, taking my mind with him (or her) flying in circles, getting lost under this page, walking in rings like a show-dog or running direct as a quarter horse, performing under my gooseneck lamp, this creature, almost too small to qualify for the term, who has my full attention as he (or she) flies straight into the bulb and vanishes like Empedocles on Etna or a kamikaze pilot or Kipling's Ghazi unless what I think I see is him drop down and reverse back out, if it's really him, or that's him swanning about my desk, touching every surface, paper clips, manuscripts, pens, hand-mirror and anthologies, and I realize I'm the only person ever to have seen him, certainly the only one to have noticed or written him down, taken him seriously as if I loved him and that he'd only mattered to me who noted his little expert moves, his death and maybe resurrection.

The Garden Center

Why do I sense they're watching us? Everything they do is carefully planned so it looks natural. Out of sight their roots communicate with each other. They have long memories, like elephants. Some are even said to live forever, but since they rely on calcium to produce electricity and not, like us, on sodium and potassium, they move slowly, very slow so as to seem not to move at all. This protects them. We must have had a common ancestor or, since it is clear they did not spring from us, we must have sprung from them. We still share hemoglobin, and for the same purpose, to transport oxygen. When hurt they keep quiet. They do not want to be discovered. I was thinking all this "in vacant or in pensive mood," walking along an empty street, when I heard behind me a sound like the clicking of aspen or poplar leaves, then a slow rhythmic slapping like wet wide leaves in a wind. I turned. Nothing. Resumed walking. That noise again. I moved to the side to let it pass. Nothing. Perhaps it was my trouser cuffs, so I hoisted them up and continued on my way. But the noise followed. I went quicker. It did too. I slowed down. It did likewise. I turned a corner and waited. The sound grew closer preceded by a floral scent until a woman in a flowing green dress, a wide-brimmed bosky hat on her head, flowed slowly by on loose rubber flip-flops. I let her pass and get almost out of sight. Then I followed her to the Garden Center where I lost her again in the medicinals. I looked about until I made her out among the exotics, fig trees, potted palms, palmettos, aspidistras, and the like, standing under the heart-shaped leaves of a rubber plant, *Monstera deliciosa*. If I'd had the means I would have bought one. Instead, as I was leaving I stole a handful of walnuts to feed to the squirrels.

Ontological

I'd watched God blow kisses through the furnace door He'd flung open for my father. I wanted to wave. Instead I tried to call him one last time, the way birds call in dense woodland. But nothing came, not even a peep, unlike birds for whom even a peep is serious. I stood there, remembering something he once told me: Never stand and piss facing the sun. Years later I found this in Hesiod, which I doubt he ever read. After the funeral I asked my wife if she'd like to go for a walk. "What's in it for me?" she replied.

Later that afternoon, taking off her glasses and laying aside *Logical Investigations*, from which she had been taking notes, she asked "Want to go for a walk?"

As we crossed the square, a small dolphin floated overhead.

"You know," I said, "I kissed a girl in Dublin."

"You've never been to Dublin."

"We agreed to meet in Manhattan but she never showed."

"You've never been to Manhattan," she said, looking up at the drifting dolphin. "How long has this been going on?"

"Couple of minutes," I said.

We passed a weeping girl and a blind man with a white-tipped cane. Both were looking up. His hands were held wide and the phrase "ontology of the open hand" came into my mind as he pointed to what he could not see. He reminded me of my father on the stairs, stumbling, falling back on me. I tried to catch him. I wanted to tell him something. I wanted to explain. When I die there'll be no one to do this for me.

"Let's go," said my wife.

That morning over coffee which, my wife reminded me, was Husserl's favorite drink, she said she had a dream of her mother.

"She's not dead," I said.

"That's beside the point. It's a dream for her who cannot dream."

She got up slowly and walked over to the window.

"In a garden there were three old ladies. One was carefully painting the shadows of flowers, another came up and offered me three overripe greengages on a china plate, then my mother pointed to a long line of birds on the horizon and asked me a question I can't remember. Her voice was like bells."

Invention

"I like your shoes," I said as she came down the steps and stood beside me, as if it was our first date, which it was. I liked her smell too. Not her scent. That was something she put on. Her smell, what she is, a kind of abstraction, an essence.

"I like your scent," I said.

"I'm not wearing any."

We started to walk, holding hands, the fibers of whatever brown animal she was wearing rubbing off on my navy-blue pea-jacket.

"You know," I said, "the most memorable thing in my life?"

"Yes, singing in the Tallis 40-part motet. 'Spem in alium' in a cathedral, and you an atheist."

"Yes," I said. "I don't need God for wonder."

"Yes, what's God got to do with it?"

"Tina Turner? Tell me about the pampas."

"I've told you."

"Tell me about your horses, your gauchos. Anacondas. Indians. Did I tell you I'd always wanted to be an anthropologist until I discovered they had to measure skulls, and I'm rubbish at math?"

I waited for a reply, but when I looked down my hands were swinging free, and all that was left was a trace of fragrance, new-mown hay, volatile, like a sound that wasn't there and which I had to invent.

Mnemonics

It's raining again. Little information is getting out, and that conflicting. I swing between optimism and despair, wondering how long this will last. I think of Defoe, cataloguing, recording. I think of Boccaccio's seven young men and three women diverting with stories, one a day. Some days I'm fearful, stomach an empty pit, mind unable to remember even the simplest things like my zip code and phone number. Forget the Zoom I have to learn for remote teaching. Logical process is beyond me, rational structure unavailable. I feel ashamed of myself, my life, remembering my father five years at war, battling the North Sea, dodging U-boats, evading mines, Stukka dive-bombers. Sometimes I think I should put myself out of my misery as I attempted to do at age fourteen, throwing myself off my bicycle at high speed only to tangle my legs in the chain and pedals resulting in bad bruises and a sprained ankle. When I tried to correct my suicidal technique a few years later I was rewarded with a concussion and two hip pins. No, I had no success in that direction, but temporary loss of consciousness has always been one of my ways out of suffering. Sleep is my alcohol. I'm almost falling asleep as I write this. I "self-isolate" and "shelter in place," as if the virus were a crazed gunman. I heed instructions, or at least I did until today when, although we've been told to stay out of gyms, which are closed anyway, I decide to go for a work-out. There'll be no one there, a crummy place run by the city in what was an old public bathhouse built in the '20s. So off I go, careful to obey "social distancing," which I do in the normal course of events anyway. I am not a social being. I climb the steps to the former Women's entrance which is now the entrance for everyone. There are big locks on the big doors but the keys are either lost or somebody forgot to lock up since, though a notice says "closed," it isn't. I turn and look back and down to the small plaza. Nobody. But there on the wide bench surrounding the thick flagpole and flag at half-mast, which it always is, under the notice "No Dogs Allowed. Respect The Flag," I see the head and shoulders of a young woman at one end of the bench and out the other the bushy tail of a dog. It's New York. It's not impossible. After all, I've always accepted the idea that mermaids could exist, not to mention the resultant mutants from a nuclear blast or maybe even a new virus. Now, before I go on and recount my adventures at the gym at a time when everything could disappear if not with a bang then a whisper, thanks to the Chinese habit of eating bats or pangolins, I have decided to remember and leave a record of as much of my life as I can, just in case, you never know. Trouble is, however, I have a bad memory, therefore I have devised a system of experimental mnemonics to keep things straight. So, for example, if I want to remember that someone said "it's a nice day," I reduce the phrase to its initial letters: IAND, which then becomes "I am not dim." Thus the result of even a short incident or brief dialog could be condensed into a narrative that might appear as nothing to an outside but to an insider, in this case me, when back-engineered, should be clear. It's a bit like a court stenographer whose single taps turn impossibly into proceedings. But, you might ask, why bother when all could go *poof*? Well, hope springs eternal and I recall someone saying that if Dublin should disappear, as might well happen, it could be reconstructed in detail from Joyce's *Ulysses*. Thus, if the same fate should befall Manhattan, as might well happen, at least that small part I deal with daily could be reconstructed by means of the following vignette demonstrating social milieu, class, even race and so on. I'll start with the gym where, stretching on my tacky mat, I hear the following which I later transcribed from my code, starting YMKH, or "Yes, Magic, Know Him." From this mnemonic, my memory kicks in and comes up with a full transcription, which is the following: "Yes, Alcindor too, the Bronx. A girl-friend's sister still thanks me. Magic axed her to go to the hotel with him but I told her hell no, he only wanna do you. She still thanks me, man, 'cause after that he tol' everybody he had the AIDS. You saved my life, she still tells me." I sit up. "I knew Bill Bradley," I say. "I sold him a car." Now I'm doing my inside thighs and the guys are talking snow, how there wasn't any this winter. "Ice is bad too," I say. They look around as if they don't know where the voice is coming from. "Snow, yea. You get trapped with a woman you don't like—." "Even if you do like her." "My brother-in-law jumped out a second-floor window and landed in a snowbank, but that was far as he got." "I got double hip replacement, pins and two new knees," says someone on a stationary bike, slowly pedaling backwards. I finish my workout. Back in in the changing room I'm squeezed between two men who continue talking as if I wasn't there. "Public defender?" says the man with cornrows. "Fuggitaboutit. If you ain't got no money fuggitaboutit. You have to steal." He looks at me. "You a lawyer?" "Sorry," I say, "I'm—." "On probation," he tells the other man, who says "me too. They're sending me upstate for panhandling." "Musta been more than that," says cornrows. "Well, maybe for jumpin' turnstiles and public urinatin.'" They both laugh. "That in the subways will get you sent up anytime." Now here, dear reader, I have to make a break and admit that while the above transcript or translation started out well it soon became clear I'd have to fill in a few gaps, which does not, I hope you'll agree, detract from my method's usefulness and efficiency. To get the drift, and work out the rest for yourself, I'll append the rest of the story in the code I described when we started out, so, here it is:

Keys

The pandemic is well underway now, and essential services such as hairdressers and nail salons are shut. My cardiologist had said my irregular heartbeat, mitral-valve prolapse and dilated ascending aorta prohibit exercise, but all I do in the gym is stretch, no heavy stuff. I go get my lock and key, but the key's missing and I can't find it anywhere. So I set off for the hardware store a few doors down and stroll along the shelf displaying keys, old and new, arranged in groups but not by any helpful system I can ascertain. On a lower shelf I find three large glass ashtrays. In the first is just one key, in size and shape clearly inappropriate for my purposes, in the second is a small collection of miscellaneous keys a glance reveals to be less than promising, while in the third keys are piled up and hanging over the rim. This might well prove to contain what I need had I the time and patience to sort through, compare and select. This whole thing is getting out of control so I do what I should have done at the onset: give up. I return home to exercise if not physically then mentally and in this most unheroic of times return to the *Odyssey* via a new translation since over the years all my efforts to learn Greek had proven as unsuccessful as my efforts to find a key. So I sit at my desk reading the part at the end when Penelope opens the door to the storehouse where Odysseus keeps his bow. I am struck by the description of how she inserts the lock and "shoots back the bolt." The mechanism has me puzzled. I try to make a drawing, but nothing looks right. Perhaps Homer himself (or herself) had lost the secret of how it worked and just made stuff up to sound convincing enough. After all, to most readers, it probably isn't important how the lock operated. What was important was that it did.

Perhaps Homer didn't want the suitors to know in case they got inside and practiced with the bow on the sly, who knows? Actually, if they'd really wanted to get inside they could have jimmied the lock and covered their tracks. Amphinomus, in particular, seemed a pretty clever fellow. As I muse on locks, I recall that James Joyce was another clever fellow who had fun with the insertion of keys in locks. Then there was Casaubon and his search for the key to all mythologies. I go into a daydream sitting at my old maple desk into which, over the years, I had scraped, scratched and carved whole landscapes complete with non-existent stars, impossible constellations, comets and meteors above a landscape complete with towers and cloud-capped pinnacles, fortified walls and parapets, ladders going nowhere. I'd take out my penknife and absently continue the story until what my eye-doctor called "ocular migraine" compromised my sight: long or short strands of beautiful drifting lights, not lights but shapes that looked geometric but weren't, threads bright as magnesium flares against dark smears, flowing, receding into nothing. These are shapes you think you make out, but can't, as they drift away, towards, sideways. If you try to anticipate their movements you're wrong, same if you think you can follow them when just anticipating a direction affects it. And what eyes are you using? They're there with your eyes open or shut; they are seen beyond sight and have nothing to do with sight, bedded somewhere in the electrical folds of the brain. They defy light, they defy dark, they defy our physics, you feel they'll never go away, though you try to lose them by looking out the window at dusky clouds, where, through it all you think you can make out the sharp shape of a duck flying right through the lights that slowly give way as the duck slides through them, and away out a corner. Perhaps the duck is the key to focus the whole thing.

Avatars

They've closed the "meat-processing plants" across the country, JBS, Tyson, Smithfield and the rest. Workers are getting sick, carcasses are piling up and rotting, animals are slaughtered and buried or just left to fester in feed lots. The "supply chain," we're told, is "breaking." So Trump issues an executive order to open the plants. But how is the "very stable genius" going to effect this with his thumpish flatulent signature? Prop up corona-ridden workers in front of a huge carcass and command them to cut, hack and hew, fit great beasts into plastic slabs? Why not?

I was reading over the above paragraph in my journal just after I'd watched a documentary about a veterinarian whose job it was to get semen from a buffalo. Before this, I'd assumed that something as important as insemination, even in our industrial age, was conducted in the old-fashioned way. As I watched the various preliminaries, my mind wandered to when I was a kid. Whenever our bull was serving the cows, there was my pal, the excited ten-year-old Michael Dunleavy, running through the streets shouting "Come and watch the cows get fucked! Come and watch the cows get fucked"! His mother and her friends chased, yelled, but could not catch him. We only had one bull, friendly and calm but also quite old and unenthusiastic. The men had to coax him to mount, help him in, then whack him on his rump to drive the point home. But that was not the method of the vet on TV. She had the bull driven into a narrow metal box where his head was gripped in a vice to keep him still. Then, pulling on an arm-length plastic glove, she shoved her arm up his ass all the way to her shoulder. She wiggled her arm back and forth until, judging the moment right, she withdrew it and stuck something the size and shape of a small torpedo back up, in and out, until an assistant, who had been holding a giant condom in place to collect gobs of semen, deemed it sufficiently full. The sodomized buffalo, noble tatanka, was then released and stumbled off looking, to me, rather puzzled.

    Why do I relate this? Perhaps because of a vision I had. recently, the kind where I have no way of judging degree of probity or conditions of circumstance. I was walking down the street when I saw a man in a shop window transferring a large drop of what looked like semen the color and consistency of Elmer's glue from a glass pipette to the end of a long stick. He then took it outside where a cow was held immobile and handed the stick to another man who drove it inside the cow, in and out, while she bellowed like a ten-wheeler going downhill without brakes. Finally, the cow's eyes clouded over and her head, neck and spine with reproductive organs attached came away, enabling the procedure to continue in a manner more streamlined and in a more convenient format. When done, head, neck and the rest were sewed back into place and the cow released, making way for the next one. People walking by either ignored what was going on or laughed and joked as they may or may not have done ages ago at ceremonies centered on, for instance, Io, Europe, Pasiphae, "cow-eyed Hera," and other avatars of the Moon.

Boots

While the Norwegian lecturer is answering a final question from the gallery, and doing so in great detail, I realize that the voice from the gallery and the voice from the stage are one and the same. He must have taken his lecture very seriously, I think, to have gone to the trouble of recording those questions for himself to answer, and timing everything so exactly. He finishes the question period with a joke in Spanish which breaks up the audience but which I fail to get. I don't even believe the audience does either and are laughing just to be polite. I decide to laugh too. Haha.

Next day we had intended to start spring break, but I have to delay it a couple of days when I remembered a visit to the dentist, who does what she has to do. "Do you want this?" She holds out to me a folded sheet of bloodied tissue paper which she opens. To show appreciation, I look, affording the kind of attention to a rotted molar that I would have given to a part that had once performed a vital function, a heart, say, or a lung. Then "No thanks," I say, "you can have it." "If you're sure," she says. "We use them again for implants, bone granules from cadavers, specially processed, of course. The whole thing fuses to new bone. You sure? You never know, you might need it later." I take the proffered packet and stick it in my pocket.

I am wakened by the cooing of a mourning dove on our air conditioner. It keeps turning its head to look at me. I get up and prepare for our trip to the seaside. "Let's kill two birds with one stone," says my wife. "I need my wellington boots mended. There's a specialty cobbler near where we're staying. The soles are loose. Very select clientele. He has a special technique based on a special fire." She pulls on the wellies though the weather is fine, and off we go on the bus. "Oh, I do love to be beside the seaside," my wife sings softly to herself. After checking in at the hotel, we search for the shop to do her repair work. Eventually we find it down a blind alley and are greeted by a little man with a heavy foreign accent and an even heavier foreign name. After my experience with the Norwegian I don't trust him. Wogs begin at Calais, as my father used to say. In any case, my wife takes off her wellies and the man goes into the back where we can see him maneuvering them over lively flames. I tell my wife I'm impressed she knew of such an esoteric repair man, and think how she must have many such secrets, secrets I don't want to know. The little man brings the boots back. She puts them on, smiles and takes a few steps around the shop. I note that the soles are still a bit loose and now flap as she walks. I tell her so, but "they're perfect," she says. "Just what was needed. Or good enough. I'll take them." The man retrieves them from her and puts them in a plastic bag which she hangs from her left arm as we walk. I carry what I am carried by would have made a good riddle, I think. "Aren't you going to wear them?" I inquire. "Oh no," she replies. "They're much too good for that. Here, you can carry them. Let's walk along the beach." Since walking along the beach would solve the problem of her being barefoot, I agree. I take the bag which she soon retrieves and runs happily ahead, hopping onto a breakwater the tide is flowing over. Suddenly she disappears. I look around. People clamming, people fishing, just people. No one seems to notice anything unusual. I walk over and search for a clue. There's a faded sign that says something but nothing relevant. Is this another of her secrets? I look for clues on the causeway and drop down the other side of the breakwater onto rocks. Two uniformed policemen are there fishing. I explain, but they know nothing.

"At least," I say, "if you're not interested in finding a woman you might at least show some interest in finding her wellingtons." They look at each other. They don't fool me. "Have you seen a large plastic bag?" I persist. The bald one says "For, like, a drop-off?" Who does he think he is, secret service, under-cover narco cop? "Finding people requires a steep learning curve," says the fat one. "Didn't I see you," I ask, "at that Norwegian's lecture about how the universe is guided by the principle of maximum diversity so it unveils itself in a way as interesting as possible?" He could have been under cover. They look at each other again. Have I found them out? "Not us," says Baldy. "At least, I don't remember. I have a poor memory. Now, what was it you came over for?" I tell them again. "You should have more self-respect," says Fatty. "In the old days we'd lock you up for talking like that, after duffing you up a bit. You sound really careless, losing things. And just coming over like that, you make it hard for us." They look about. "Aren't wellingtons uncomfortable?" asks Baldy. "I don't wear them," I reply. "Perhaps you should," says Fatty. "Make a man of you. Big boots, them." He pauses. "Maybe something caught her eye. There's something here that doesn't add up, something we're not seeing." "Maybe something's afoot," says Baldy, and laughs at his joke. They both look at me. "You say she just repaired them?" "Well," I reply, "they didn't look repaired to me. I just went along." "There you are, then," says Baldy. "No wonder she took off."

The Ukulele

Walking from my office, not for the first time I heard a flapping sound in time with my steps. I looked about, up, behind. Nothing. As before, I thought it could be my cuffs scraping the ground, so I hoisted my trousers higher and continued on my way. But the sound followed, *swoosh, swoosh, swoosh*. I pulled my pants still higher. A young woman passed me wearing loose, soft flats like carpet slippers. They may even have been carpet slippers for all I knew. Yes, that was it. It all seemed a bit déjà vu, I thought, walking on. Then that sound again. I decided it was in my mind, or it just wasn't anywhere. Either way, I'd live with it.

I was soon in the market where I went straight to the steamtable and swiped two sausages, which I ate as I toured the noisy aisles. On my way out, I took a handful of walnuts and dropped them in my coat pocket for the squirrels. In the park I called out "George"—I gave them all the same name. Two ran up, a black and a gray. On hind legs, grasping my fingers for balance, they accepted the nuts, taking them in their teeth, and scurrying off. I still felt their touch, even as I wiped my hands on my trousers.

As I walked back to the office, I became aware of that sound again, now more like the *whoosh, whoosh, whoosh* of those giant wind turbines they'd installed near my summer place, driving down slow crows and real estate values. I was lucky to get out when I did, but the locals, a dozen families related many times over, who sat on all the boards, making rules and fun of what they called "weekenders," those of us whose taxes paid for most of their amenities, well, those locals made a bundle from land sales, construction costs, kickbacks and the like. The whooshing didn't bother them. I imagine they even liked it. What did they care if those screws that dwarfed the *Titanic*'s pulled in the entire valley, a cow, a horse, a migrating flock? Most had taken their loot and migrated to Florida.

Well, by now lunchtime was over. I'd almost forgotten about that *swoosh, swoosh, swoosh* and was concentrating on how to avoid my boss, a snake of a man who made a habit of landing on his feet in jobs he couldn't do, who terrorized the women with his "attentions" and followed us all around with his eyes. I would like to kill him. Yes, I would if I could get credit for the act without being held accountable. I'd do it. For nothing. I was greeted by sounds from his office, him practicing his ukulele, something he often did, *plink, plink, plink*. He was supposed to be quite good at it. The office ass-lick said he could even discern Vivaldi in his repertoire. I wouldn't know. The only ukulele I knew was in George Formby's deft ditty, "with my little ukulele in my hand," which was supposed to have a double meaning, though I wouldn't know.

Krum Marisje

A penny whistle, not tin, but dark wood. I play in my sleep. Fingertips find the small holes and a tune grows, simple but firm, lively but delicate. I play until I'm sure I have the tune by heart, and when my wife wakes I play for her, the same tune, again and again, but now with more twirls and tremolos, even a furbelow or two, though I'm not sure she likes it and perhaps is just being kind when she applauds. In any case, I hum it when I get up, I copy it down. Even Mozart copied down the music he heard in his sleep. Nobody taught me. Just the pipe itself taught me how to rouse it with fingertips, blocking and releasing air, weaving a tapestry of breath, a blanket of simple sufficiency. The tune is still with me as I walk over to my old Corona and begin to tap the keys, enjoying the clatter, the force that makes words when it hits the page. After a while, however, it is all too much. It can get on your nerves so all you want to do is escape, anywhere. I rush to the closet, drag out my father's battered brown cardboard suitcase, toss in my whistle wrapped in brown butcher paper, add socks, toothbrush, and stuff. When I get to my amour's building, however, I realize I've made a mistake which there's no way of repairing. Still, I get into the rickety metal elevator, bars rattling, and alight at the top floor. Her door is open but the place is empty. I should have made my intentions clearer. Suitcase in tow, I back out, call the elevator which rattles and shudders as I get in. It descends in jerks, at every floor, ignoring the "T" I keep mashing. It finally grinds to a stop, a stop determined primarily by the fact that it has reached rock bottom, which is really a figure of speech because there is no rock here where Krum Marisje, once stood, if "stood" is the right word for Little Crooked Swamp, since a swamp is variable, responsive to time and weather; its roots are mud, and you can sink in. But here a clean, swift trout stream flows in one side and out the other, rippling like flute music which I bet could have got on people's nerves as it rattled over rocks, split light so as to dazzle and confuse the eye searching for an elusive silver trout disguised as water. I drag my suitcase out of the elevator and head home, wondering if it will still be there, if my wife will be there. If not, at least I still have my pipe.

Voice

In the *Historia Tolteca-Chichimeca* it says "The god of duality is at work, creator of men, mirror which illumines things." That was true then, no doubt, but now, though we may think the same thing, we phrase it differently. We say things like the age of the universe is ten to the power of thirty-nine, off the charts, ungraspable, so old the idea of age is meaningless. Some experts also say that the universe is a self-excited system brought into being by self-reference, which is, I suppose, something I can relate to since it could mean I go about my days as collaborator in a participatory universe which gives birth to consciousness which gives meaning to the universe as an endless series of receding reflections in a pair of facing mirrors each taking from the other what it's taking from itself. Yes, I say to myself here in the bathroom, I can relate to that; that's one way of looking at things. But how far does it get us? I need a fresh voice, new, simpler. Some pass by, kicking up dust in their eagerness, making me cough. *Fresh*, I said. I keep trying. I need to start from scratch, *ab initio*, so to speak, right here and now, right where I sit, on the face of it a very unlikely place, to be sure, I think as I reach down and pick up a book which a house-guest must have left, Justinian's *Codex*, in which he attempts to put his house in order. I flip through the pages. Maybe I can pick up a hint, you never know, but breaking in through the door from time to time is the voice of Cardi B on Instagram: "Let's say I have the coronavirus now, OK? How am I supposed to know I got it because sometimes I be like 'if you have a cough you got it?' OK?" And so on, getting worked up and interrupting my meditation. But, yes, a voice, not dusty paper, something alive and deep as Tuva throat-singing, whistling overtones and subharmonics, aryepiglottic folds vibrating like demented butterflies, slowly drifting to *bel canto* ringing me like a bell, making me hope "my bowels shall sound like a harp." But just when I think I might be getting somewhere there's a knock on the door and I feel like a fool just sitting there, forgetting what I came for, still waiting to complete my business. I might as well be sitting on a deckchair on a beach in Florida, kicking back, or in Alaska on one of those self-decomposting units they have there, very hygienic and forward-looking. Then another knock, louder, a banging, and a voice, "Is *anyone* in there?" Good question. I get to my feet quickly. Justinian falls to the floor.

Ghosts

I went to sleep thinking of roasted cherry seeds and the German girl I'd seen lifting her skirt near the Templo Mayor, and then I was crossing the canal that led to the brackish lagoon, rain stippling the surface on which a few marigold petals shivered, and a floating flotilla of dead monarch butterflies. A boat was coming from the other side, and the festival behind it lit fire after fire so the whole place burned like an unhealed wound, and we passed, saying nothing, specters, older than the surrounding mountains, father and son, and as I turned to watch him leave I saw something like a thread pulled from a spool, so it unraveled from both of us and caught me in its toils so for a while I couldn't move and when I did I was a phone hovering over his bed, waiting for him to die, but before he did he called and told me to go to hell, which I did.

At the Museo

Sleek as a mirror, still sharper than my new razor, it looks hungry just lying there on its new bed, *feed me, feed me*, the obsidian knife, the eternal child, *tecpatl*, son of Cihuacoatl, *Lady of the Snake Skirt*, mother of all, who opened her womb and dropped him from the sky and when he got lazy she herself came and walked among the people dressed in white with him swaddled on her back until she left him in the market place where a woman would find him crusted with gore and get the message and rush him to the emperor who knew what had to be done and soon the twin staircases sang with repaid blood and the skull-rack swelled. As I look through the glass at what is glass itself I see it through my own reflected face. When I get home, I take from its cardboard box my pocket-knife of best Sheffield steel, "Radiant," with mother-of-pearl handle, reclining unused on its cottonwool bed calm as Manet's *Olympia*. My father gave it to me, as his father had given it to him. I take it everywhere I go.

Nanabush

The past is more present than the present, most of which will never make it to the past so there will be no time since everything exists at the same time. Time is just intensity in a world playing tricks, so, for example, the house I grew up in is still there though deemed "of insufficient architectural merit" and demolished for town houses which the neighbors now protest for blocking their light. I ignore what had or had not happened and wander in the waste lot that used to be there, picking things over, sorting through like that rag-picker or the rag-and-bone man who gave you a goldfish in a jam-jar for stuff you brought him. I came across a weather-beaten card that read "Follow Your Heart," which reminded me that my father died of a heart attack after a life of congealed beef-drippings spread thick on bread like butter, which has made me watch my own heart since he made me clean my plate and swallow all the fat I cut off. He wasn't made of money. It didn't fall from trees. My mother told me that on his death bed he told her to tell me he loved me. Good for him. My angina sounds like a girl's name. I can watch my heart dying on a device. It seems impossible, a bit of a joke, as if I'd been tricked by myself, like Nanabush scared at a noise behind him so he kept spinning round and round, finding nothing, deceived by his own farts.

The Universe

From above it looks like a shiny cigar with holes along the sides. The roof has yet to be filled in but this will be done before it leaves its berth. There is not much activity and little noise. It will all happen when ready, everything having been carefully planned by that man standing beside a large computer, his fingers relaxed on the console as if playing a harpsichord or organ. The man on a stool to his left is wearing goggles as he looks down and files his nails. His thermos sits on top of a blueprint sheet of instructions. Two men are squatting on the left wing, the only one completed. The man with a Mohawk is gazing into space. The one with the buzz-cut is looking at the metal rafters. On each side of the ship are signs saying UP or DOWN or NEITHER. There are also signs with red arrows. Everybody knows what they mean. Desks and computers line the walls of the hangar but there's no one at them. Green, red and white wires are strewn about and yellow squares are outlined in tape on the concrete floor. A dolly stands empty at the bows near where the ship is tethered. A woman is starting to paint on the fuselage black and yellow stripes like a queen bee. In the far-right corner of the hangar another woman is crouched over a flight simulator that is at present of little use but is intended to approximate the current weather, wind contours and pressure configurations. When all is complete, a trip will cost a bundle, but the stated idea is to get as many people as possible into the *idea* of space, if not into space itself. It is the brainchild of a multi-billionaire, a self-described "humanist" who owns at least one island in the Caribbean and who wants everyone like him to have "a transcendental experience," to see "the wonder of the universe up close" or as close as one can get. An intimate friend of his, a renowned scientist, in anticipation of great things was, before he died, in the process of inventing a genetically altered tree to grow on comets and generate a breathable atmosphere. This man is also generally hailed as the author of the idea that the universe is guided by what he termed "the principle of maximum diversity," guaranteeing that it "unfolds in a way that is as interesting as possible."

Recording

I point the camera up the embankment at the top of which they now seem to be going so fast you can't even see their wheels spinning. I can barely keep up with my long lens and can hardly make out that they are so many snakes. This has never been filmed or photographed before. There have been all sorts of stories, all kinds of accounts reported, but on examination none has stood up to scrutiny. All have proven to be something else, some peculiar atmospheric effects, some unusual weather conditions, all so rare as to be unique, and simply some pure lies or fabrications. In any case, there I was trying to keep up and just as I was following them around a curve, watching them go into a tunnel and out, I was reminded of standing with my father on the footplate of "Mallard," recently crowned holder of the world steam speed record. It had come to our station to be inspected and admired after its triumph. We joined the line, and once on the footplate pulled levers, read gauges, looked into the empty fire box in what was the only intimate moment I had with him. So far as I know, "Mallard" is still there. I think it may have been the first thing I ever photographed with my Kodak Brownie. Be that as it may, there I was furiously following the procession, the ceremonial peloton never before recorded. It shot ahead, but I followed, put in a spurt and caught up as it passed through a small town. I got so close I didn't need to adjust my close-up lens and couldn't believe what I saw: The large green snake in front had a smaller brown snake in her jaws, a kind of *Pietà*. I feared she was about to devour him, but slowly a white cottony stain like diphtheria spread from her jaws. I knew I had to get this, the pinnacle moment, so I steeled myself for the instant when her fangs would sink in and the young snake would just hang there. But no. That wasn't the point at all. As her jaws closed slowly, the stain drew back like the tide and the young snake stirred, stiffened up, filled in, looked about. The transfusion, the transfiguration had taken place and I had it all. Though my camera was full, it kept recording. It kept on humming. I couldn't put it down.

The Event

"Quite the choreographer," I said as she took a step to the side, passing without touching. She smiled and opened the fridge, which was strictly partitioned; the same food either side. Talking was not encouraged, so I smiled back and shut up. You could talk, but only if what was said was relevant to the situation at hand and aided the purpose we were there for. We occupied the same space without dominating it, which took skill and concentration, not to mention luck, in order to avoid physical contact in the constrained space of two bedrooms, one bathroom and one kitchen. With light from the open fridge illuminating her, she turned, kicked the refrigerator door shut, gesturing that she was going out with her two children, a boy and girl, twins. I too had twins but they were with their mother whom I had intended to call earlier that day but I was out of slugs, "gettoni" as we called them when I was growing up in Nemi, in the Alban hills above Rome. We were only allocated a few, most of which I soon used up, but hung onto some to use as we got nearer to the Event, or the "Coming Out." You never know. The crisis had come and gone, but there was still the future to take care of. Meanwhile, it was time to visit my bed-bound mother. Gathering up supplies and whatever else I needed, I set off, letting myself in and stepping carefully down the ill-lit stairs at the bottom of which she lay in her windowless chthonic room, reading by the light of small lamps whose batteries it was my job to check and, where necessary, replace. I also had to keep an eye on the Growlites that fed pale but still fecund colorless sporium flowers. I bent and kissed her forehead, emptied the chamber pot she kept under the bed, replaced and folded the cloth she draped over it. My mother taught me everything I know. Now she was on the way out I hoped to become everything she was, within reason and natural boundaries, of course. Or perhaps not. In any case, the epidemic had made many changes necessary, and some things had changed on their own. I knew my mother was proud of me, though she'd never say so. The streets were coming alive again, a sense of hope gradually taking hold, though we were all wary of excess. I was one of the few still required to wear face coverings and took it as a mark of distinction. I made my way to the church, now largely cleared of its function as hospital (though what is a church but a hospital for the soul?) and made my way toward the sanctuary where a doctor and nurse were waiting for me, greeting without touching. I took off my clothes and laid them under the altar as I had when, after stiff competition, I was chosen for investiture. The check-up did not last long, but it was far from perfunctory. Photos and x-rays were taken, and compared with those taken earlier, as in a dentist's office. Measurements were made of, for example, the angle of incidence whose ideal was as close to zero as possible, as vertical to the sun as could be and as flat against the desired plane as necessary, inscribing a golden section. Finally, volume and distance were calibrated, and a sample taken with an electric probe. When done, the doctor thanked me as she replaced her instruments in their boxes and the nurse said "cometh the hour, cometh the man." But I was only doing my duty, repaying for my accident of advantage. I made my way home still swelling with pride though I knew it goeth before a fall. I had been chosen not just for the dimension of my ambition, and the beauty of the instrument to effect the desired result, but also for having cast farthest even with my eyes shut.

 A week or so went by and then, one day when I returned to the apartment, my co-tenant was nowhere to be seen, all signs of her gone, so I knew the time was close. When they came for me the following Sunday I was ready, though not quite prepared for what I saw in front of the reconfigured civic center near the park, where a crowd was growing. At the top of newly constructed stairs in front of the reconfigured civic center there she stood, green from top to toe, headdress a bouquet of interwoven flowers, breasts pushed out and apart, a skirt wide and flounced. People parted as we approached, but now, here, before I continue, at this point I should point out that the events I am about to describe are not widely known, or if known not widely understood. I pass this on to straighten the record and aid anyone who might wish to emulate us, though matters of such import are known properly to minds prepared. 'Meaning' is felt integrally and rightness is measured by the pure heart's integrity. Someone once said that "what cannot have happened is nevertheless thought," but this doesn't go quite far enough. Thought and action are, to us, in the light and nature of our recent experience, the same. The 'meaning' of all this is shared amongst us, but not with outsiders who would doubtless misinterpret what they thought they heard or saw. Without like-minded participants who could understand, for example, the activity of a priest celebrating Mass with its body and blood? And what mischief could misinterpretation lead to? So we decided to close off our town and post guards, though no one could guarantee that, like the virus itself, some outsiders had not already made their way inside. This was probably how the rumors started in the first place, though there were already in our midst cynics, sceptics and nay-sayers who could have been responsible for the various misinformation. Others there were who dubbed our proceedings a mish-mash of paradigms and New Age fantasies, but what we intended was a return to simplicity of body and health of soul; not a return to pre-virus existence but a re-birth to what, indeed, may never have been but which, since it could be imagined, had to exist. We intended banishment of division, shame and guilt, the reinvention of sacrifice as donation, the transformation of a simple, ubiquitous and yes, even vulgar act into a realm of the spirit, flame rising from slag, as wine from blood, or to take a different tack, in the words of one of our leaders, organized religion today is fossilized into big political parties. We have become blind to the mysteries of life and death. Yet still the divine is a legacy we all inherit, and secularity, even if for some reason desired, can never be achieved because we are haunted by a sacred prehistory which it is our duty, no, our salvation to acknowledge and renew. We intended the creation of a new kind of symmetry, not only the connection of left to right, male to female, and so on, but patterns on larger or smaller scales, the way of the self-similarity of a broccoli flower echoing branch and stalk, the sunflower spiral echoing the spiral of Andromeda, an order on different rich scales. Have long is the coast of Maine? It depends on scale, and since details have details, the process goes on, maybe forever. Now some people have claimed that our whole venture is conceived in the spirit of irony. But even if it were, isn't irony itself bracing and, like comedy, a power of healing and renewal? Moreover, as a great philosopher once said, "every concept is framed in its own irony." Well, be that as it may, I return now to my narrative, to the Event.

    I walked with my escort of young men and women to the public park where a dais had been newly erected beside the reconfigured public library, white with a red roof. The young women took off my outer garments and handed them to the young men who arranged them carefully on the ground. Almost as naked as the day I was born, I walked up the steps to meet the Handler who led me through the large doors that closed behind us. On we walked down the long, dark corridor until, deep in the inner sanctuary my remaining clothes were removed by invisible hands, and my body anointed with scented oils. Then I was turned around and led back out the way we came, out into the light which momentarily blinded me when the two large outer doors were thrown open onto a brighter, chillier spring day. Gently, two young women, the Hand-Maids, all in green like the Handler herself, slipped their hands under my arms and led me forward before they stepped back. I was left alone in front of a silent crowd to discharge my obligation and meet my fate, which I did gladly. The way up and the way down, I remember to have been told, are the same, even though the way up requires the fusion of will and native spontaneity, body and mind, while the way down is the concomitant response to a deep and natural force. To swelling applause, at the hands of my erstwhile roommate I rose to the occasion, erupted a rich, sparkling parabolic arc that embodied the rising promise of the post-pandemic, a new time, deliverance, before falling slowly like fireworks. And now I was getting chilly, feeling curiously sad, but soon recovered as I looked out over the crowd. I could have sworn I saw trees greener, birds louder, women plumper, old men younger, young men livelier. The Handler was drying her fingers on a silk cloth, having rinsed them in a gold-rimmed bowl the size of a chamber pot.

Enlightenment

"Stop! I only want to ask you something."
 I stopped and turned.
 No one, but I had already learned that the absence of rose defines "rose." Same with "no one."
 I looked again but couldn't make him out clearly though I knew he was there, if only as "a diffuse multidimensionless configuration" that didn't fool me. It was as if I could smell and hear him at once. But it was more what his absence suggested than anything he gave off.
 I kept walking, thinking I'd given him the slip but then, suddenly, there he was right in front of me, his pals off to the side. He seemed to be their leader though it was clear that what he said was influenced by their presence.
 He asked again.
 I tried explaining, but with no luck.
 They had their own agenda, though it was not at all clear that they had not confused me with someone else. Or it was as if they thought me a hat and were trying me on for size. In any case, they took me down a side alley and beat me up, leaving me unconscious until one of them returned to tell me they weren't the ones who did it, before dragging me off and leaving me on a bare heath, nothing all round. There I lay under the stars, ever the optimist who believed "everything happens for a reason," and as the mists cleared I recalled how a Zen master would bring someone to enlightenment by smacking him upside the head or throwing him off a bridge. I knew enlightenment was wordless. True, I was thinking in words but thinking is silent and therefore kind of wordless. And then it hit me, I was enlightened!
 I hobbled back to the town whose lights I had seen dimly see on the horizon. I knocked on a door.

"You look a right mess," said a woman. "You should clean yourself up."

I tried to tell her what happened, that I was enlightened, but words would not come through a mouth caked with blood. I doubt she would have believed me anyway.

Coconut Oil

The small arena was not even quarter-full although this was a world-title fight. My fighter was out front talking to her friends and family. She had insisted on wearing a bikini top and bottom, which were fetching but hardly appropriate. She wouldn't go on without them. Her brown skin shone with coconut oil, which, as her manager, I had protested as too culinary, but to no avail. She was the champ, after all. She could do or wear whatever she wanted. As I looked around the curtain, I could see she was now delivering some sort of speech. I listened, and discovered that her topic was "Love," a diagram of which she had outlined on the blackboard behind her. "Love," she said, "is—." I couldn't make out the rest but I did observe that the remaining crowd wasn't paying much attention, and her opponent was playing cards with her second in the corner. Eventually, the referee rang the bell for round one, my fighter climbed under the ropes into the ring, the two antagonists met in the center of the ring, touched gloves, sparred a bit then, suddenly, my combatant dropped, deliberately or not I couldn't tell. I carried her backstage where I administered fluids and massaged her carefully, careful not to touch her inappropriately. You can't be too careful these days. You never know what you're going to be accused of. Soon she sat up, thanked me, and went back out into the fray. The other fighter was still in the ring talking quietly with her manager and debating what to do next. Then both went over to the referee and argued with him though he seemed to be having the better of the discussion, pointing out that though it was true that my fighter had quit the ring, according to the strict letter of WWBC rules, before a fight can be considered over, the opponent's manager has to be consulted or informed, and he—pointing to me—has done neither. I made myself scarce, not wishing to get involved. Those remaining in the audience, however, mostly my fighter's family, were treated by her to the rest of the lecture on "Love." The air hung heavy and fragrant with coconut oil, infusing something almost religious.

Sportsmanship

I'm not in the lead but somewhere in the front, loping along a narrow path through woods, by fields, but when I come to a clearing with a small house I stop, remembering that the rules say that if the path goes through a house you have to go through too. No deviations, no cheating. I am about to run through the door which runners in front have opened when something catches my eye. I look up to see a fellow competitor jammed into a high window, trying to unstick himself. Was he trying a short cut? Did he mistake the path? Was he cheating? Perhaps I need to rethink my route. I decide to run around the house and rejoin the path at the other side. This hardly constitutes cheating. If anything, it takes longer and I am handicapping myself. I feel I am accommodating my plans to the situation at hand. So I continue running through woods until I approach the town and hop down a series of steps to the finish line, which actually isn't a line at all but an open door into a kind of workshop. People are milling about and look at me blankly when I inquire if this is the finishing line. Eventually an old codger with a set square in one hand and a ruler in the other says the line is where it is. Such tautology cuts no ice with me and the place does not look promising, so I leave and jog over to the shop next door. Ah, a large blackboard with names and numbers in chalk. I move closer, eager, push to the front but in the process trip and brush against the board, smearing everything so little or nothing can be made out. I guess I came in somewhere near the front, though I could be wrong.

Nowhere

They were cleaning the place up, pulling the old japonica out, though I liked it ragged and overgrown. They were moving about like they owned the place. As I lay on my bed in the room by the front door, they trooped by in ones and twos, threes and fours, looking in, waving as if they knew me. I hated them. They were taking over, encouraged by my parents, mostly by my father who had been trying to get me out of the place where I had lived my entire fifty years. Now he was in his element; he had the upper hand in the small, crowded house. I felt his presence when I walked over to the drawer for my wallet and found it empty. I went for my bedside ashtray where I kept my collection of foreign coins and that too was empty. The hints could not have been clearer and did not even need the large young woman who entered my room, closed the door, emptied her suitcase on my bed and sat down on it. I was about to go and talk to my mother and tell her to talk to my father when there was a knock on the open door. I opened it and there she was, largely naked. "Look what I've had done!" she said, turning a complete circle. She looked like the statues and paintings of King Tut, wide hips, protruding belly. "Very nice," I said. She gave one more flounce and took off down the stairs. I set off after her, needing to talk, but she had disappeared into the crowd in the garden and was now busily raking, pruning, digging, pulling up stuff. My father, as usual, was nowhere to be seen. I knew when I was beaten. Fifty years down the drain. Time blurred, and next thing I knew I was on the street, having been evicted from a boarding house that refused to accept foreign coins for rent. I'd tried to sneak back into my room to retrieve at least something after the custodian had taken pity and let me in. But whatever was there had been piled into a corner, and even a quick glance revealed none of it was mine. On the street again I had no idea where I was, but I did know I was cold, freezing. My one coat had been left somewhere, or stolen. Looking down, I saw I was wearing slippers. I wasn't prepared for this, nothing had prepared me for this. As I wandered around city streets, wouldn't you know it started to rain, as in a bad movie. Drains started to overflow. Since I had nowhere to go, I decided to go there.

Ants

The wind was starting to whip up, scattering dry leaves, getting among my leaf pile which I thought I'd extinguished until a thin line of smoke rose, and then the sound of crackling. Flames started to appear. Water I splashed from a pail had little effect. In fact it seemed to feed them, so I emptied the whole pail, hoping for the best.

    Once started, a fire is hard to put out. I hadn't even remembered starting this one. Just then, a young man came round the corner of the house with two friends. I thought I'd done explaining the place to them though they had done most of the talking. When they approached, I noticed that the young man's eyes were filling with tears, but the trio swept aside and away and were invisible until they climbed the steps and entered the house. I followed and went in through the basement door, where I smelled something like the burnt hair of my childhood when a barber would finish off a haircut with a lighted taper to the nape of the neck, thus completing a "short back and sides." As my eyes adjusted, I made out various small animals hunkered down, as if they had taken refuge from the wind. I bent to scoop up a pigeon squatting like a carved decoy, but I couldn't get my hand under it, the way I had as a kid reached under for a hen's eggs. They'd all have to leave, despite being spooked by the wind outside and the smoky pile visible though the open door. I cautiously approached a dog who was sniffing the dust until he'd cornered a crowd of ants and lapped them up. I decided to keep this to myself. Who would believe a dog that ate ants?

Pops

All the lights went out in the huge barn I'd spent a fortune renovating, so much money I had none left to furnish it. And now this. I didn't know where the fuse-box was though I'd been looking for it high and low. It had to be hidden in plain sight since there was nowhere really to hide in this cavernous windowless structure. Then I spotted it up high near the dark rafters, flat against a side wall. I should have noticed it before via the clue of a ladder fixed against said wall, going nowhere but up. I had assumed it was just a decorative feature since the people I bought the place from were architects from the city. I'd come across the place by accident when, on a weekend scouting trip upstate, I was taking a stroll when I heard what seemed to be bobcats fighting. I crept up, only to discover not bobcats but two women fighting in a ditch that ran in front of the above barn. They saw me, pulled themselves together, and ran inside. Taking advantage of the situation, I followed and had soon struck a deal for the place. They hated each other and wanted out fast.

Once I'd dumped all their stuff, I had a shell, though I felt rich. My father would have been proud. But I didn't know where anything was and out of politeness had never asked the sellers. I didn't know if they'd bothered to put in any plumbing, though it turned out they had, mostly however in the most inaccessible places. The barn, after all, had been meant for cows and horses. So now there I was, wandering about in the dark, having to figure out how to get at the newly-discovered fuse box accessed by a ladder that didn't look too safe, seemed to be insecurely attached to the wall and went on forever. Why, I asked myself, had they made it so difficult to get at? To keep it away from who? So up I climbed, slowly, cautiously, the ladder shaky and creaking. But I made it and reached out to flip the switch. Suddenly the place was awash in light from bulbs scattered about and recessed in all sorts of nooks and crannies. I was about to stand up in triumph, but thought better of it, which was just as well because right at that moment there was a *pop*, a series of pops, and all the lights went out. And there I was, high in the dark, hanging on like one more day survived.

The Dog

I'd just moved into this small apartment after my divorce. I call it an apartment but it was really just one small box (the bedroom) inside another L-shaped box (the living room). There was no kitchen and only one small window no bigger than a letterbox. The shared bathroom was down the hall. Here I'd done my best with whatever furniture I found on the street, none of it in great shape, and I wasn't sure where to put it to best effect. So I called in a buddy and we moved stuff around in what space there was, put it here and there, stood back and discovered everything was back where it started. It would have to do since time was short and I was about to start a new job.

When I did start, nobody seemed to notice my arrival and no one gave me instructions. I wandered about, free to leave, it appeared, whenever I wanted through the large open gates of the warehouse adjacent to the factory. But I chose not to. Instead, I walked among the looms, chatting with the factory girls, cutting through the cigarette smoke of the men. In this way I spent my first day until the whistle blew and the machinery growled to a stop. Some women now made for a huge table piled with extra pieces of cloth and chose whatever they wanted, holding them up against their bodies, toward the light, wrapped themselves in bolts and sheets before staggering out the gates and home. Other women went to a long table laden with fruits and vegetables left over from the daily provisions and carried away as much as they wanted. I wasn't sure if I could do the same, so I didn't, but when I saw my ex-wife on the street I alerted her to what was available and she dashed in.

When I returned to my tiny apartment, I'd hardly sat down on my one chair when I heard through the window a squeal of brakes, a scream and yells. I got up and looked out, and there she was. I thought that perhaps the police had caught her shoplifting since she was laden down with scarves, dresses, pinafores, a bolt or two of cloth and so on. But why was she bringing them to me? I had no time to complete the thought because the commotion had been caused by a dog, lying there on the sidewalk. Why would a responsible owner allow a dog to run about loose on the street? A small dog, too. I squinted through the smeared window and managed to make out that the poor beast had on a collar, a metal tag, and a bell. Much good that did it, I said to myself. How unjust everything is, I thought, remembering as a boy standing in line at a counter with three grapes in my hand, wondering how much candy that would buy, looking at the sugar-coated jellies which I knew were out of my reach. No, she wasn't bringing them to me. She walked right by, stepping over the dog. Things just weren't right. Things just weren't fair. Things just didn't add up.

The Case

My neighbor has convinced me I had a case for infringement of intellectual property and persuaded me to let him file an action. It didn't seem much to me, a few footnotes from a short paper I published on hydraulic engineering, but he was persistent. "From tiny acorns mighty oaks do grow," he quoted from somewhere, and I gave him the go-ahead. Which led me, a year later, to a packed two-tier courthouse with everyone in face masks and a harried judge who kept sipping what I assumed to be water from a tall wine glass. As people were piling in, a fight over seating broke out below me. A large woman was battering with closed fists a man's bald pate. His friends, trying to deescalate the situation, were holding him back, thus making it much easily for the lady to deliver her blows. Between batterings, she glanced up and caught my eye. I tried to look away but she made a tight fist gesture that reminded me of my sister whom I hadn't seen in decades. Then she returned to her altercation with renewed vigor. My sister? My shrinks don't last long, but they all agree that my problems are rooted in my inability, or willful refusal, to dream. "In dreams begin responsibility," my most recent shrink said, but I told him I didn't know what that meant. Responsibility for what? And how does that help? My problem, I think, is that my day-to-day life seems rather unmoored, disconnected, maybe even dream-like, perhaps. For instance, I've always regarded as a memory, as fact, that my father took me aside at about age ten or eleven to explain human reproduction. The whole process seemed rather illogical if not unnecessary but I listened, and when I told my sister about our "talk" she said mother had done the same to her, though she was a year younger. She too was unconvinced. "Show me," she commanded. I did. She looked, grabbed and squeezed. *Ow!* She squeezed harder. *Ow!* Again. "Now you," I managed, more in the spirit of fairness than in the adventure of knowledge. I couldn't believe what I saw, or didn't see. No way in, no way out. We left it at that. But as I sat in the courtroom, a place devoted to truth, I wondered: Had that really happened? Had a dream made it happen? What did it make me responsible for it if had? Had a dream stopped me dreaming? My current shrink keeps hinting she wants to ask me why I never married. Now that's a question I regard as too intrusive to answer, but I do get to wondering what my sister made of this, if—but it's none of my business. Besides, she lives in another country, married to her work as an emergency room nurse, overwhelmed, probably, by the pandemic. Incidentally, the judge never got to our case. We have to return at a later date.

Wimps, or What the Monkey Said

"Now this one is different, and I'll tell you why."
   "Why?"
   "Look over there. What do you see?"
   "See?"
   "How about that guy on a skateboard, flying about?"
   "I mean—."
   "Where's he going? What's he doing gliding through empty warehouses, skimming over a city crammed along the banks of a large river, in and out of empty houses, factories, docks, crumbling staircases, storefronts, through walls as it they aren't there, people as if they aren't there, and many aren't."
   "That's impossible."
   "Could be."
   "I mean, on a skateboard?"
   "See for yourself. The air looks like an ocean, so maybe a surfboard."
   "And he goes on, for how long?"
   "Exactly. But there's a twist. I'm not sure that young man is really him, though he might be. There, now he's left his board and, in a more hopeful scenario, is following home that lovely young woman from her English language class."
   "It reminds me of *The Ghost Sonata*."
   "He's slipping behind pillars trying to keep out of sight. He's even stepping round a lush patch of stonecrop, careful not to step on the beautiful yellow flowers. She goes into her family's restaurant and disappears inside."
   "Have you read Strindberg?'
   "You see how now he's decided to hide in the arcade in front of that empty storefront and wait for her to come out. There's faint music somewhere, can you hear it?"

"How's he know if or when she'll come out?"

"He doesn't. He's hopeful. He's playing the averages. Anyway, I'm not him, how do I know? I'm just telling you what I think he's doing. I may be wrong."

"I was just—."

"Hang on. He's facing one way, the way he expects her, so he doesn't see her brother come up behind him and—."

"And what?"

"Do I have to do all the work? Look for yourself."

"Well, I really can't see what—. It reminds me of—."

"Let's take a time-out and reconsider the situation. First, do you agree that you can't see most of the matter of the universe, it's invisible?"

"Do I agree? Who am I to agree?'

"Good. Now we know this invisible stuff consists of giant cosmic clouds of subatomic particles flying around doing things. Do you know what they call this stuff?"

"How the hell—."

"It's called 'wimps', short for weak something or other left over from the Big Bang. Those wimps drift through the world, through everything, nothing stops them, not even us."

"You mean people have seen these wimps?'

"Not exactly. They're still looking for them but we know they're there."

"You seem to know a lot."

"You don't have to know a lot to know a lot."

"That's not logical."

"Logic? The dance of those impotent to create. The abolition of memory.'"

"What happened to the girl?"

"That, as the monkey said as he peed into the sugar bowl, remains to be seen."

House and Garden

I was on my way to visit my old house again, walk around the flat field stones I'd placed in two circles, one inside the other, between them soil I'd made from table scraps, tree duff and dung from the back field, and in that soil planted fragrant wild thyme, dug from that field. When I got there, however, those circles of thyme were now a pond of great depth and amazing clarity at the bottom of which I could see a spring bubbling with grains of white sand rising and falling, pulsing. This pond drained slowly off to one side and flowed uphill, past the house. I followed, watching small trout flashing and twisting in and out of shallow places, over and around rocks. When the stream reached the quarried top of the hill it snagged on itself, sending spray up and off, moving as if still, balanced in its flow like bolts of silver cloth until, bursting its banks it cascaded in a long fall. Surprisingly, I was not surprised. This was the reason I had made the stone circle in the first place. It spoke to something beyond itself and, as I stood there, hands in the bright water, I recalled my ancestor Robert Boyle, who engaged in the physical world in pursuit of abstract truth. He plunged his fingers into dung, watched quicksilver fizz in his palm. He believed colors could be differentiated through texture. Thus, black was prickly, "as if you were feeling needle points," and red was "very smooth." I was trying to imagine what blue felt like and wondering about white, "no color, nothing but nuance," as I followed the stream back down to the garden where I knew, suspended in the darkness of soil, fruits hung from humus, umbilicals hummed and globes floated like planets, pushing up and out, deep rhythms, mouths open like fish rising to air, great bulbs of suns to hold in your hands, spheres floating up into the altiplano, orbs sinking down to depths, delighting in their utility. Back at the house, I noticed a wasp dragging a cricket up the cedar siding, getting half-way, dropping it, retrieving it, starting again, the process continuing until and again until I closed my eyes to a sky so clear I could see right through to the other side where I watched a wasp dragging a cricket up the side of the house, only this time I could hear the wasp's curses and grunts, the cricket's cries and screams. Above, a great bird was leaving marks to be read like the afterimage of a flame.

Brian Swann

Structuralism

I had just left my office and was crossing the parking lot near the church of St. Jakobus when a kid on a skateboard came from behind me, hit my right shoulder and spun me around. He stopped, looked back, laughing. I ran up and knocked him down so hard he planted his face on the asphalt and lay there spread-eagled. Well, not really. That's what I would have done if wish were father to the fact. In fact, I watched him ride off and was still planning revenge when I arrived at my grandmother's flat for my weekly visit when I would chat and administer Ben Gay, which she called "Ben-Hur" from the last movie she saw. After her usual complaints and comments on my lateness, she lay back, hoisting her dress and pinafore rather too high. I began massaging the adductor of her left leg, noting again how smooth her skin was, then moved to the sartorius. She let out a yelp and cursed. I apologized. After I cut her toenails she made me pick up each clipping. These lunchtime visits often left me uneasy, so I always planned something pleasant afterwards. Today I thought I'd arranged to meet my wife outside the art museum at about the usual time, but when I arrived she wasn't there. I waited before deciding to go into the large exhibit of masks and maps, whole corridors of cartographies, each one blown up, expanded, sometimes high as the ceiling. Many pinpricks of intense yellow light shone through the paper or fabric, defining, outlining, illuminating, but in the process often blending borders and limits. This was confusing to anyone who was not so much interested in the fractal geometry of nature as in its regular ordinary details such as coastal configurations, deserts, steppes or mountain ranges, not to mention towns and cities as parts of political entities. As I negotiated the exhibit, I realized that what I was seeing was not so much made new as rendered unfamiliar, which has its value but I would have liked to have known how it could have all been made to cohere, how all apparent disparities could have been made to come together even if only as binary possibilities, which would have been comforting. I was walking along, mulling these thoughts over, when I realized that I was going too fast and, if my wife was behind me, I could outpace and eventually lose her. I slowed down, but if I went too slow, the exhibit being so large and complex, demanding close attention, she might well overtake me and neither us realize it. Of course, if somehow she was already ahead of me, she would likely keep going hoping to catch up but in the process miss me. I needed an exact equable pace to effect the desired result without resorting to algorithms and the like. So I reduced my pace and sat down on a bench by a window, taking from my briefcase a bottle of apple cider vinegar I sip for stomach troubles, just before a fellow art-lover arrived, sat down beside me, and took from his overcoat half a dozen miniature vodka bottles, the kind you used to get on airplanes. Lining them up along the sill like soldiers, methodically he knocked them back in sequence, one end to the other. I stood up and looked out the window, across where the store fronts were occupied by semi-naked young ladies, or life-size cardboard reproductions of same, it was hard to tell, which may have been the point. Replacing the vinegar bottle in my briefcase, I continued on my art museum educational tour, but gradually came to the realization that I was feeling the same way as when I began college all those years ago: What you came to learn they assumed you already knew. This suited me fine and saved everybody a lot of unnecessary trouble. Even then I believed in the universal properties of mind, synchronous totalities. It was no great leap for me, therefore, in my sophomore year to major in anthropology, specifically structuralism whose coded meanings proved that all recollected experience, even history itself, is contemporaneous. This meant that I didn't have to go traipsing about in foreign parts doing "fieldwork" and risking horrendous ailments and viruses, not to mention having to measure skulls. So I stayed at home usually finding what I was looking for except, as in the case today, my wife.

The Egg

He was painting over the wall again, red as the barns hereabouts whose paint they used to mix with oxblood. You could still see the old layers and shapes, palimpsests he'd painted over before and which others had painted over before him, that high brick wall, higher than he could reach, stretching away either side. I watched, offered no help. Didn't he realize they'd do it again? You could live here generations and they still wouldn't accept you. Maybe he did realize this, but by now it was a family tradition. The locals scrawled and tagged, you painted over, and so on. It was almost as much a cultural phenomenon as The Egg which I was carrying, though perhaps I needn't have bothered since the ceremony had been cancelled this year because of the virus. I needn't have checked to see if the egg had been strengthened by boiling, but when I did I saw one end had cracked. Perhaps I'd held it too close, gripped it too tight. I wasn't sure I'd done the right thing by taking it in the first place. Should I return and slip it in its usual spot in the wire tray under the counter? Someone might still find a non-sacramental use for it, especially since the grocer was also the bus driver and knew lots of people from all over, some of whom I could see across the street waiting for him to arrive, start the engine, and get going. But he could have been in the store waiting for an order to arrive, so I decided to wait until the coast was clear. In any case, I doubt the egg would be missed, or even if it was, it would be back in its place, waiting for another year, not unlike the egg in the Birdman ceremony on Easter Island. Anyhow, I walked back the way I'd come, past the wall-painter, and once home dialed 48459. She'd know what to do. Nothing. I called again. Waited. Same. Perhaps I should call another number? Instead, I called the same number, despite knowing that to do the same thing again and again after failure is a definition of madness. But this time, success. I asked if she still liked eggs. She was Armenian, long beautiful nose, long beautiful face. With a history of genocide she'd know what to do, though I didn't know her that well. She may have come from another story, even one I haven't written yet, maybe one I never will, never get a chance to in the Age of Covid. In any case she didn't want an egg. She didn't even like eggs. This got me nowhere. I'm still stuck with the egg which I doubt will last a year till the next ceremony, even if there is one. If it's so important, why doesn't the egg itself somehow let me know what to do with it? This is not what I signed up for. This gets us nowhere. There has to be more to it than this, a shadow disappearing round a corner, just as there has to be more purpose or meaning to the virus that produced this crisis, that little packet, three strings of RNA just 3000 letters long, "bad news wrapped in protein." If only the egg could hatch, my problem might be solved.

Cold Feet

Vivian and I were discussing the end of the world, something we often did these days, and which, given the state of things, we regarded as inevitable, if not immanent. We decided that viruses and parasites would undoubtedly play a role in this process. As a language buff, I wondered about the words themselves, and suggested that "virus" had something to do with Latin *vir*, a man, but Vivian disagreed and the ex-lawyer in her set off to find the truth via Google. "'Poisonous fluid,'" she announced. "If it has anything to do with man it could refer to poisonous masculinity." She then googled "parasite," informing me that the word meant "close to food," and we were the food. From there we drifted around, taking Google to worms and nematodes whose biomass in all our bodies, it said, would equal 8000 elephants or 500 blue whales. We also learned that the horrendous tape worm can grow to one hundred feet in a blue whale or break off bits and live forever, even in us. When we found ourselves among pinworms, to lighten the atmosphere I tried to tell the story of how as a child I'd stick a finger up my ass and watch these tiny white creatures wave about, dancing like angels on the head of a pin. Vivian wasn't interested and brought our discussion back to the virus, the kind that isn't even alive until it hijacks a host's cells. The idea made me shudder. I stood up. "What we need," I said, "is that vacation we've been planning, to get away from this all." We set off a few days later, farming out the dogs to neighbors.

As we left the hotel, I could hardly see out the rear window of our rented Bentley. We did not travel light. Why should we? We were on vacation, a time to escape, spend some hard-earned retirement funds, and do as you liked. So off we set again, but the streets were crammed, especially what they called "high streets," I don't know why. I could discern no difference in altitude. Having to drive to the right did not help matters since left and right seemed arbitrary with small cars dodging here and there and double-decker buses going wherever they felt like going. Why they even had such huge buses, let alone huge trucks ("lorries") on such narrow roadways eluded me. Many was the time I aimed for a space, closed my eyes and hoped for the best. I must have been born lucky, but the constant starting and stopping, braking and accelerating was taking its toll not only on our nerves but on this expensive automobile also. There was no right of way. Traffic came from all over, even small blind side streets. By the time I made it through I was a wreck, and Vivian was too. She was also hoarse. Plus we realized we'd lost our phone. Not at all what we'd planned for a long-anticipated vacation. When finally everything opened up, however, we were surrounded by the lovely countryside we'd seen in travel books and brochures or on TV, e.g., *Escape to the Countryside*. On we drove, until Vivian said, "Doesn't it all look the same?" I looked and, truth to tell, she was right. We'd been on one long road with no traffic. "Where's the map?" I asked. "Map?" she replied. Skies lowered, a little distant thunder. I glanced at the fuel gauge as we passed a whitewashed building from which a faint "Amazing Grace" emanated. "Perhaps," I said, "they'll know where to find a gas station." "Petrol station," Vivian corrected. I pulled over and we got out. Silence. "Perhaps they're all praying," she said. "It might be rude to barge in." So we set off again until, a mile or so down the road I noticed a house, white picket fence and all. Beside a low wicker fence, among roses and hollyhocks, a tall man was talking to a couple. "They might know," Vivian suggested. I pulled over and got out. "Welcome, welcome," the man said. "Once I've finished with these lovely people, I'll be glad to show you round." He looked at the jam-packed car. "I see you're all ready to move in." He laughed. Who could resist such a kind offer? We got out, took a deep breath of fragrant air, stretched our legs, followed him inside and looked around. It was as if we'd stepped into a travel book. There were large paintings on the wall, many of them, judging by the costumes, dating back when. There were old books open on old tables, wood (oak?) beams, period furniture and lush carpets. "Would you mind awfully going back and taking off your shoes?" the gentleman asked us. "Socks too if you feel like it." Then he turned to the couple who had preceded us and ushered them, barefoot, up a wide staircase, followed by a large tabby cat. We wandered sockless, admiring everything we saw and feeling quite at home, comfortable walking about wherever we pleased. When the man and woman had been escorted down and away, the gentleman came over. "So do you like what you see?" "Oh, oh," we gushed. "Good," he said. "And so, would you like to make an offer?" "An offer?" "For the house—the property out back is extra, of course." We began to explain how there must have been a mistake, and outlined our circumstances, to all of which he listened politely. "Of course," he said, "an easy mistake." He accompanied us to the door where I was about to put on my socks but the cat had mumbled them soggy. Since driving sockless in shoes would feel unnatural, and even perhaps prove dangerous, I decided to drive barefoot, despite Vivian offering her argyles. On we drove, but after a while of interminable countryside I felt we were getting nowhere, an opinion shared by my wife, who broached the idea that since we were about halfway there we still had the option of turning back. "Halfway where?" I inquired. She shrugged. For some time, Vivian had been worrying about those high-jacking viruses, which was what she was thinking about now, I surmised, when, giving me a strange look, she sat back and closed her eyes, tight. I kept mine peeled for an open gas/petrol station. Then it started to rain and what had been a passable if narrow road became a narrow track with no banks at all, hemming us in. And when it really began to pour the track became mud, and we found ourselves at the bottom of a steep hill, where I stopped the car and looked about through bleared windows. Vivian opened her eyes. Two other steep muddy tracks converged with ours and both of them looped back the way we'd come. Our only chance was to choose one of the three, which was really no choice, all being the same. But we had to settle on one, factoring in the fact that the gas/petrol needle was now on E and my feet were very cold.

The Reception

"To shut our eyes is travel," wrote Emily Dickinson in a letter. I shut my eyes, but when I opened them I was in the same place. I read his name tag, "Clyde Howe," I said. "Are you," I asked, "by any chance related to Curtis Howe?" "Curtis? I am not," he replied, looking over my left shoulder. I waited for more of a response but none came so, knocking back the last of the cheap Sauternes in my glass, I continued my saunter among the trays of small cakes and sweetmeats, picking up a tart here, a piece of pie there, something more exotic from another plate, by which time I had forgotten both "Curtis" and "Clyde" and was wondering again why I had bothered to come. Receptions were not really my thing. You went about making small talk, looking for the main chance, checking out the women. I looked about for someone to tell my story to, make my pitch, though if someone had told it to me I wouldn't have believed it. I'm fully aware of the figure I cut. From his response, it was clear to me that fellow thought Curtis was a man when in fact she was a woman. Was it in his interest to lie? Was he telling me to keep my distance? What did he think I had in mind? What could I have possibly wanted from him? The arrogance! The presumption! I strolled around, more purposefully now. You'd have thought that at a literary gathering they'd have had something appropriate like a tray of madeleines or even a plate of cheese, "the ghost of milk," as Stephen Daedalus called it. Maybe Wordsworthian Wensleydale. But no new land here, no new expanse to explore. Pocketing a handful of petty fours, I took my leave. *I will turn their house into a junkheap,* said a voice as if from a foxhole, a voice I knew well. Again, I consoled myself with empty threats. I sat on a bench, closed my eyes and bit into a pastry.

Brian Swann

Retirement

There's more room in my office, he said. Just divide it up properly. Five could fit in there with me at least, he said. There's no need, I said. Now you've retired, no need for you even to be here. But where would I send my saplings, my books, the cases of wine? he said. Send them to your house, I said, like the rest of us. My mailbox is too small, he replied. They clutter up the place here, I said, and you don't even bother to pick them up. When I'm in town I do, he said. But that's the problem, I said. Did you know your aunts are in trouble again, he said. Don't change the subject, I said. Up to their old tricks, he said, but they haven't been caught. Same old false trail trick, he said, with candy wrappers Then the hop over the fence. When are you planning to pick up those trees? I asked. By the way, he said, did you know Ray's back? He can go back where he came from, I said. He leaves for years without a by your leave then comes back and doesn't let me know? Call that a friend? He said he'd tried to contact you, he said, but you turned your back on him. Let's, I said, leave it at that. I never did and I'm deeply hurt. He never even told me he was going. But, he said, you knew where. I'm surprised he came back, I said. Maybe it wasn't his choice, he said. Ever heard of revenants? In any case, he told me he met Eddy Plunkett there, remember him? Though not Gloria, whom he'd left to marry an architect. Together they renovated Dunsany Castle and he took up the title after his father's death. They had two sons, he said. Sweet guy, I said, wandering about painting those boring abstract canvases. Anyhow, don't try to change the subject again. What? he said. I said don't change the subject. When are you going to pick up your trees? The leaves are down, they're falling apart. We're going to need your office. Everything is as you left it, and if you give us your new address we'll try to send things on, including your trees. Small saplings, he said, but too big for my mailbox. And you know my address. It's been the same for a while and will probably be the same forever now I've retired.

The Fourth Wall

It was very kind, especially since I hardly knew them, but in those days that's what people you met at a party did. "Oh, you'll be in Paris/ London/ Rome! Wonderful! We love Paris/ London/ Rome and keep a place there. You'll be welcome to use it. Here's the key." And that was how I found myself staring at a long, high, wooden wall of cupboards with sturdy knobs. Each cupboard had a large keyhole for which I had no key, so I was planning to use force, expecting some resistance since there were deep grooves and scrapes in the wood where, presumably, someone had tried to jimmy them open with a crowbar or claw hammer. I yanked one knob and, to my surprise, the door opened easily. Same with the others. As I peered into each compartment, they seemed deeper and larger than their outsides suggested. Most shelves that lined the sides were empty but others were stocked intermittently and, I judged, without a master plan. It was a hodge-podge at worst, a miscellany at best; no gathering of like with like or even unlike with unlike. Some compartments were long and capacious, others more like cubby-holes variegated in size and shape. After my long journey, I was hungry, but instead of searching for something to eat, curiosity won out and I walked along, cataloging in my mind what was and was not there. Sometimes I reached deep into empty dark to ascertain if at the back there was anything that had been forgotten and found a few transparent receptacles with rice, oats, beans, different herbs, as well as an assortment of empty vessels with labels peeling off. I could have concocted a bite to eat, I suppose, and was thinking what might go with rice when a bright package of instant noodles caught my eye. Perfect. Now where's the sink, where's the tap? I looked about: two walls, to left and right, plus the third wall that made up the front of the long cupboard. Where was the fourth wall? I knew it was there, I could sense it, if only as the result of guesswork based on an expectation of rational structure. But perhaps, I thought, its design was deliberately inconsistent and variable, and maybe I could work all of this into my doctoral thesis on stylologistics which I'd come here to avoid because it was giving me so much trouble with models that were hard to replicate, not to mention difficulty locating what was lost in the "represented." Then, as I looked about it slowly dawned on me that there might be a way to deal with the essence of stylolinguistics not as altogether a problem of abstract logic but perhaps as a way to address the vagaries of choice and guesswork, incorporating what had previously not been properly considered, such as what could exist beyond the fourth wall, given half a chance.

Brian Swann

Landskip

There were salt hills.
There were sand hills.
There were salt and sand hills, a lot, here and there, while in the distance a mountain range roamed, so lovely, so Sangre-de-Cristo-rose in the evening, so pueblo-light in the morning picking out peaks, vermilion, carmine, maroon, emphasizing crannies and crevices so the contrast made the salt hills blindingly white, sand hills warmer, ruddier, cinnamon. Yet salt and sand still seemed out of place, as if it had been placed there deliberately, provocatively, to make the observer long for them rather than just have them provided. As it was, they did look as if they still needed to stretch beyond themselves to be on a par with the mountains; they needed to aim beyond description so they wouldn't seem out of place, something to be accepted without thought or question. Yet they certainly provoked questions, such as who would leave such hills, especially the salt ones? Were they a by-product of anything, some long-forgotten industry or one still on-going but hidden, out of sight? As for the sand hills, what is sand a by-product of anyway? Could the whole thing be a left-over Hollywood set? Could the mountain-range itself be a by-product of something, maybe paper-making, papier-mâché production, the crumbling and piling up of sheets to see what they'd look like or be good for, egg cartons deconstructed and exaggerated? No, that range had nothing domestic or industrial or tentative about it. It could have arrived out of nowhere with a mind of its own but it looked now as if it had always been there thinking its own thoughts. The same could not be said of the sand and salt hills which looked accidental, tentative. To be sure, the mountain range may look a tad

histrionic in certain light, but it stretched perfectly from side to side, carefully proportioned and arranged.

Brian Swann

House with Smirr and Lummin

"They don't want it anymore," he wrote, "so I thought you might be interested. Enclosed please find photos of the improvements they made." I'd always regretted selling it, and only did so because I couldn't be bothered to make changes and repairs, installing a new roof, for instance, removing the black mold growing on the wall near the ceiling, meaning to get a dishwasher for the space near the sink and a medicine cabinet for the upstairs bathroom, not to mention fixing a crack in the garage floor and not knowing what to do about the split in the grain of the pillars holding up the deck and how to deal with the green stain in said pillars when I discovered it was an arsenic preparation. These pillars, each the size of a tree-trunk, went straight down into the soil, making me afraid the weight they supported would prove too much and everything would come crashing down. And then there was the guard rail loose and twisting to the side and the deck that needed staining and the house that needed painting inside and out, windows that needed cleaning, and on and on. Best use and leave, I'd decided, which is what I did, but now as I looked at the photos and saw that all the problems I knew, and probably more I didn't, had been taken care of, improvements made so that the old original structure was almost unrecognizable, a more complete version of itself, I began to feel the emotion that had drawn me toward the place initially, perhaps even more intensely, so it felt almost fragrant, that warm place tucked into the forest on the side of a mountain, at the end of a red dirt track.... Yes, I wrote to the real estate agent, I was interested, and to myself I said: you can start again, leave this city apartment floating halfway to the clouds. Why had I stayed here so long when what I do can be done anywhere?

But traveling up on the train I began to have doubts. Whatever made me want to buy a house in the first place, and having got rid of it why buy it again? I was becoming more than a bit confused also because in all the years I'd lived in that house I'd never taken a train to it. I wasn't even aware that a line went to a town anywhere near. What would have been the point? As I looked out the window, I still wasn't altogether convinced I was doing the right thing, even when I stepped onto the empty platform, tossed my bag over my shoulder and set off in what I hoped was the right direction. After what seemed miles, I stopped and looked around. It had started to drizzle, and I was beginning to think it might be a good idea to turn back, assuming, of course, that I could find my way back. I took out my map which was soon soggy and difficult to read, took a few steps and—and there it was! I had arrived! I stood back to get a better view and make certain. Yes, my house, for sure, no older, no newer, shining in the mist we used to call *smirr* in Scotland. I looked down and around. Yes, roof tiles scattered in the deep grass. Then up again. It didn't really look like the photos I'd been sent, somewhat changed, perhaps, but not to the extent the real estate agent had claimed. Same problems. I climbed the tilted steps to the deck where the screen door was still hanging on one hinge. I pulled it aside and opened the unlocked front door. Actually, it never had a lock that worked. I found myself in empty space, the floor covered with leaves and detritus as if bears had made a den there. The rooms had been somewhat rearranged, a few rooms that were upstairs were now on the ground floor, and vice versa, and there was no way I could see of getting upstairs. The tall windows were the same, but where I had looked out and over the tops of pine and maple now there were no trees, just large rocks, and way below them a wide long lake, calm and reflective since the rain had stopped and the sun come out. Nowhere was there any sign of people, just a landscape, what they used to call a landskip, fresh, pristine. Even through the windows I could smell sweet odors so I almost ran through the glass, and out. Instead, however, I exited conventionally, plunging into the greenness, away from the house, scrambling up and down slippery boulders, sliding down slopes and clawing my way up, no plan at all until, tired, I stumbled upon a house overlooking the lake. As I approached cautiously, two middle-aged men waved and invited me inside where they informed me that they had recently bought the place sight unseen after reading a lovely collection of stories set in a place remarkably like where they were now. "We walked into a story," said the elder gentleman, who introduced himself as George. "Stories can take you anywhere," said his companion, who introduced himself as Claud. I was beginning to wonder which story I was in when Claud said, "The author was Belgian, I believe." "Yes," George added. "Henri something. He had never ever seen a mountain, let alone a lake." "You know, said George, who looked a bit like Derek Jacobi, "on second thought I believe the name sounded somewhat Mexican, like the writers we love, Arreola, Elizondo, or, or—." "Monterroso," Claud called out. "My favorite story, 'El Dinosaurio', has only one sentence: '*Cuando desperto, el dinosaurio todavia estaba alli.*' Brevity is the soul of—." He was about to rush over to a large bookcase, but I managed to bring him back to the matter at hand, asking them about my old house which, it turned out, they did not know. Just then it began to rain again, heavily, what in Scotland we call *lummin*. Claud looked out the window and began informing me that they were beginning to regret their decision to buy since whenever it rained heavily, which it did often, the side of the mountain behind the house turned into a torrent, a waterfall, sweeping around the house as if to wash it away. "We are all so temporary," mused George. "We are reluctant to move and leave, cut and run, because this place chose us, we were chosen for it. But we'd never sell." "We chose it for its view of the lake," Claud interrupted, "which might soon be filled to overflowing, and then where would we be?" Then, as quickly as it had started, the rain stopped. We moved out onto the deck and looked down at the lake now flat as a mirror. George turned to me and said it reminded him of Lake Windermere. "I wouldn't change it for anything," he said. "Me neither," Claud added. I rose to thank them for their hospitality and take my leave. "I don't suppose you'd be interested in buying this place?" George said.

A Dream

I hate hearing people's dreams, and seldom, if ever, dream. But last night I dreamt. However, all I remember is being back in college, rooming with someone who has a lot of electronic equipment which I'd have liked to have learned how to use. The next scene is a large party in the same room. Everybody is dark-skinned, and the electronic music is deafening. I'm trying to nap on the sofa. Eventually, I get up and take the stairs down to the front desk to get someone to take care of things. An elderly lady in a fluffy pink cardigan follows me back up into the packed room. She calls for attention and claps her hands. "Now," she says, "who here has felt depressed?" Hands go up. "Right," she continues, "now who has felt dark self-pity or depressed in, say, the last week or so?" Again, a raft of hands. The place is hushed, music dimmed. "Good, well done. OK, now who is depressed now, at this very moment?" All the hands stay up. She turns to me. "Draw your own conclusion," she says, leaving to silence, then applause, then the swelling electronic beat.

As I said, this was a dream because when I was in college, "electronics" was a pile of 45s and a portable turntable. Also, nobody was ever asked if they felt depression or self-pity. I'm not even sure those terms existed. You just got on with things. We working-class boys with aspirations were too busy being driven by fear of failure to even think how we "felt." We did our best in high school (e.g. the "County," see earlier) doing our best to deal with institutional and physical violence. As one example of many I adduce Bertie Blows, freckled, red-haired, slight, unathletic and ironic, son of a farm laborer, who more than once for talking had his head bashed against the desk until it bled by Mr. Watson, our German teacher. I myself frequently felt the birch and rod, had my sideburns pulled up until my toes barely touched the gym floor, and more. There was no recourse but to suffer and be the better for it. And look at me now. Depressed? No, well, a bit. But look at Bertie Blows, now a distinguished church historian and bishop in the Church of England. I could go on and on, but won't. Instead, I will tell a story of my friend Eddy Lang, who read Law with me at university and whose obit I just read in the Times. He was the only black man in my college, son of a storekeeper from what is now Belize, who taught me the mouth-organ (I still remember the tune) and who, the obit told me, rose to become his country's ambassador to the UN, father of three girls, pillar of the Methodist church, and a knight to boot. Yes, the same Eddy who so loved local nurses he often stayed out late, long after the college gates were closed, and was forced to climb in, over the spikes. Which brings me to my college pre-med roommate who I probably should have mentioned in the dream above, though I don't think he was in it. Nick was a hard-worker and would wander around the grounds late at night reciting the names of nerves and blood vessels, muscles and bones, mnemonics he'd worked out for all sorts of medical facts. One night, walking by the gates, he happened to look up and there, outlined against the moon was a silhouette, impaled on a spike. "Eddy?" Nick whispered. Indeed, it was Eddy who, lifting up his head and spreading his arms wide, said "Were you there when they crucified my Lord?" It was another half hour before the fire brigade levered him off and down into the hospital where his girlfriends took care of him enough to graduate that spring and return home to a very successful career. As you've probably noticed, this story has nothing to do with depression because I doubt very much if Eddy was depressed. No, he just got on with things, as we all did. As for Nick, I believe he married a nurse, had daughters, and died of a heart attack.

The Castle

I'm tempted to discard the heavy bag as I hug the barren mountainside like an ibex, trying to make it to the bottom, clambering over and around loose stone walls that follow invisible contours or none at all. But about half-way down I come to realize that the signs posted are not illogical, meant to mislead, that, in fact, they indicate the way in which things had been ordered. I hadn't needed to take things into my own hands. I sit on a rock probably scraped flat by a glacier and a phrase from my favorite old radio show comes to mind: "As I cut my way through the jungle that lay by the side of the arterial road …" Yes, as indicated, the best way down would have been to enter through the castle gate at the top which, as signs clearly indicate, was in fact the bottom, the lowest floors, which I hadn't believed since it ran counter to the best practices of architecture, no matter how antique, not to mention logic, no matter how arcane. But as I sit I now see clearly that such an arrangement would in its heyday have confused any invader and surely had since the castle was still standing and, so far as I could tell, intact. So, repositioning my bulky bag on my shoulders, I climb back up and enter the main gate, joining a queue for the elevator. Down I go to the top, slowly, making a stop at a cavernous baronial hall which also seems to serve as an art gallery, food for body and soul at once, as it were. Just before the doors close, I decide to make a visit, whereupon I get lost in long corridors. I stop at a concession stand to ask directions from a large person, male or female I can't tell, black curls falling from an oiled beehive hairdo. She looks straight through me, saying nothing until, in a voice almost impossible to hear, she points back the way I came. As I squeeze into the elevator, I wonder why it's called "elevator" when, in fact, it goes as much down as up, and I decide that in the scheme of things up is better than down. "Quite an artist," says a voice beside me. I look down onto the top of a woman's head. "Oh, me? Oh, thank you, but this bag—." "I mean the way you squeezed in with it, so carefully." And that's where the story ends, showing that it's not so much that the way up and the way down are the same but that we might do worse than consider other ways of ordering experience as it presents itself to us amid the general fluid futility. This was recently brought home to me when I was looking back to this experience and remembered that when I stepped out onto the mountainside the castle was not seen, presumably lost and looming in the white, lucid, rolling clouds of mist. And I was reminded of the underground greenhouse in which I courted my wife and in which we were married, and in which we still live.

Graham Bell

I've been working on the opening scene for years and, walking uphill, was thinking about the fact I had only come up with one image: A fog thick as woodsmoke but light as cold steam slowly blown away by a soft breeze. But then, on the southeast corner of Park and 34th, beside the traffic light, in full late May sun, on my way to the cardiologist I stumbled and, dizzy, fell slowly like a burdened tree. I fainted, and came to looking about embarrassed, leaning against the traffic light. There were few people. Nobody noticed. As I sat on the ground and pulled myself together, I thought about how, on the bus here a fight had almost broken out when a maskless man got on and started eating a large sandwich. In response to protests from the other half-dozen passengers, he defended his constitutional rights as an American to do whatever he wanted. I hauled myself to my feet and crossed 34th unsteadily, repeating in my head the cardiologist's name as a religious man might repeat the name of Jesus: "Dr. Virzi, Dr. Virzi." At the guard's desk my temperature was taken, I answered questions concerning my exposure to Covid-19, and was given blue plastic gloves that were too small. In the office, I told the nurse about fainting and she told me about how she fainted on the E train and nobody came to her aid. When Dr. Virzi arrived, he took all my details. I ended up with an e-Patch kit and a heart monitor stuck on my upper left chest with instructions about what to do if it fell off. I was also given a "Symptom/Event Diary" to write in each day. Though I keep forgetting to tap the sensor twice to record each symptom, the pages are rapidly filling. When all the heart-stuff flared up, I decided to incorporate it into the film script I was working on. This was not difficult to do because all I'd written up to then was a rough draft outline, an image, a sketched-out scene and one almost complete episode where the protagonist, who is probably German but goes by the name "Graham Bell," is told by his friend's girlfriend what a total shit he is, all his lying, making things up, causing trouble. He had thought he'd gotten away with it all, but she sees him for what he is. To his surprise, he is rather relieved. As she walks away with his friend, he realizes she is right. He knew it all along. He has fooled no one. He would like to call and tell someone but there is no one to tell and besides someone stole his phone. He looks about, feeling as if he is in a foreign country, in a bookstore where there is nothing he wants to buy. There's a thumping in his chest like something that wants to be let out. Faint, he staggers outside, sits on the sidewalk. It could all be in his head but doesn't feel like it. Fog as thick as woodsmoke but light as cold steam begins to settle—and that's all I've got down so far. It could be the final scene, so all I need now in order to see how things came to this pass is to fill in the rest of the movie, work in the beginning and middle which, of course, could necessitate a new end. I will also probably change the name of the protagonist to something else, since the one I have now carries too much baggage and thus could create false expectations.

The Translator

A man stops to watch a car hit a bicycle parked at the curb in front of a house. The driver stops, gets out and starts berating the cyclist, then punches him. A woman grabs the cyclist from behind, looking as if she's trying to protect him but only succeeds in rendering him easier to hit. The man doesn't know the circumstances, so he walks away along the suburban street lined with cars. Small shops. Large houses. In those houses are families, people living together, gatherings in rooms for normal living. He came up here to take a new job, and now wishes he hadn't. He walks into a bookshop and tries to catch the manager's eye. She's busy and ignores him, walking away toward the rear. He follows. "Would you like to feature my book in the window?" he asks. "Feature?" she replies. "Who published it?" "Well," he pauses. It was in fact self-published, a short collection of love poems. "Er, Scribner's. That is, I mean the paperback is from Vantage." But the manager has already turned away. He too turns and heads for the door, feeling in his pocket for the book which now seems so slight, thin as tissue. He'd spent much of his spare time on the translation, from a language he didn't know well, in fact barely knew at all. He'd performed the task with the help of a blind friend whom he'd constantly consulted with "What's the Braille say?" The original, you see, had been turned into Braille and he'd used that as a guide for greater accuracy and authenticity. Often he'd encouraged his friend with, "That sounds good. Maybe even better than the original, certainly better than any English." He touches the book again. A new job at his age is never a good idea, and if he doesn't find one soon where will his health insurance come from? He stops, lightheaded, aware of heartbeats in his ears. He counts. Missed beats. "Palpitations?"

the lady cardiologist had asked. But he didn't know what they were, so "No," he'd replied. He misses his old job but he'd had to get away. A new start, the reason doesn't matter. That's how he got those "palpitations." And now he'd have to find a new cardiologist since the old one must think him a fool and that would add to his stress. Or maybe not. Everyone is lonely but not everyone has palpitations. "Lightheaded," Merck had told him, is a cardiac symptom, but he has been lightheaded as long as he can recall. He walks back the way he came, passing the cyclist sitting beside his toppled bicycle, staring at the ground. If he has a choice this is not the kind of thing he'll choose to remember, certainly not one he'll choose to tell. He feels his back pocket. The man on the ground reminds him of someone whose name he's forgotten.

Fleas, or The Answer

Bundling up our muddy clothes, I carried them down to the basement. When I arrived at the washing machine I paused, noticing water on the floor. Someone had been here recently. I looked about. We'd have to be careful when we left, cover our tracks. But then, I thought, when will they ever leave? What to us had been a kind of usufruct arrangement, to them had been an absolute sale. With that kind of mindset there'd be no point in trying to explain. To them, no doubt, we'd always be Indian givers if, that is, they knew that we kept returning, which I hoped they didn't. So we played by our interpretation of the rules: no alienation. We reserved to ourselves what was rightfully ours. But I put the ramifications of such thoughts aside since I needed to wash these clothes, and there was some extra urgency involved since, in addition to getting rid of mud from our hard slog up here, I had to soak our stuff in scalding water to take care of my wife's fear of fleas which, she was convinced, could live in the creases and folds of our vestments, an idea she may have obtained, as a scholar of French literature, from the life of her favorite author, Guy de Maupassant who, I recall she said, was possessed of the idea that his brain was being eaten by fleas. This conviction had an extra curious dimension for me in that her brother, with whom she was very close, was an epidemiologist with a special interest, not in bats or rats, but fleas. This interest had of late taken a rather unusual turn in that he was now more absorbed in the innate and hidden dimensions of the possibilities of fleas than in their role as carriers of death and diseases such as the Black Death. "Look at this," he'd said to me recently in his lab, leading me over to a very large glass, fishbowl-like container. Picking it up, he shook it vigorously, creating a blur, a cloud at the bottom.

"Listen!" he whispered, slowly unscrewing and lifting the lid with one hand and pushing my head down with the other. A sound like a soft breeze in cattails rose and fell, rose, and fell. Then a distant music like the song of a red-wing blackbird among the reeds, faint voices of spring peepers by a pond. I wanted more, but he quickly screwed the top back on. "Who would have thought?" he said, and I had to agree. "Now," he said in the hushed tones of an oenologist, "let's try these." He picked up another glass container, same size and shape. It looked empty. With one hand he opened it while the other squeezed a bottle from which issued a fine spray of what looked like blood. Immediately, the floor of this jar shuddered as thousands of tiny mouths opened as one, wide, like the beaks of baby birds until, satisfied, they sank back down into what seemed satisfied sleep. "Listen," he whispered, "do you hear anything?" I put an ear close, tentatively. "Nothing," I said. "Precisely," he replied. "Now look over there." I found myself staring at a large screen with hugely magnified photos of the mouth parts of fleas. I was amazed at how precise they were, interlocking components of a machine that would have pleased Montaigne, who, my wife had told me, regarded animals as automata. "It's not hard to reproduce exactly each part and make a working model," he said. "In fact I've already made more than one. I'll show you later. It takes up a whole room in the house. The hard part is miniaturizing to the point where it's functional." "Functional? What function?" "Good question," he replied. "Very good question, but science, you know, often has an answer before it has a question."

Beyond Milk

From the other side of the door I heard, "This is far older even than you." It sounded like X who I'd never altogether trusted though I did respect. I poked my head round. In the dark I made out, but could not really see, what looked like the hind quarters of a black cow lying on a table. X was cutting off thin slices and laying them delicately on top of one another. As if talking to himself, he said "There is an art to this. You only need a small piece to know it's beyond the rarest wine. This—" he waved his hand around, "will last another hundred years, way beyond me, but I will know it like no other. It is beyond name, it is beyond—*fuori latte*, as the Italians say." "*L'arte*," I whispered so as almost not to be heard. "And no *'fuori.'*" "Whatever," he said, having heard. He pushed by me with his bag of slices, locking the door behind him. *Where's he off to in such a hurry?* I asked myself, watching him hop on his bike. Climbing on mine, I followed at a discrete distance. Soon he joined a line of cyclists line abreast, stretching across the road with him at the head. His high tenor could be heard leading them in something like a hymn, singing the history of the streets and neighborhoods they rode slowly through, some in harmony, some not so much, some in tune, others not so much, but all clearly committed to their purpose. I got off my bike and followed on foot. "No need to tear down statues," said a middle-aged woman to my left. "Just sing history. Let it sing itself. It won't go away. It fits itself." She pointed. "See how the road rises to meet them?" That I could not in fact see, but I did notice the traffic opening to let the singing cyclists through. Yes, I thought, you could learn a lot by listening to them. They'd done their homework and knew their stuff. Now, if only they paid as much attention to voice quality we might be able to get somewhere with this freewheeling anthology. But what did he plan to do with that bag of exquisite delicacy swinging from his handlebars? What was its purpose? What art was he talking about?

In the Leaving

Light projects the rubber-plant across the room onto windowpanes. There it stays a while like an icon for someone, the way a religion deepens and defines itself in images. I get up and walk toward it, look through the leaves to sky stretching over the town that produces little but promises much. Thus, a pond suggests prayer and contemplation, while houses that have staircases on the outside might show how, at the same time you're going up you're also going down, how at the same time you're in the outside you're also inside, and so on. If I squint, I fancy I can see all the way to the outskirts where the artistic expression of forests that need tending gives way to real terraces against which vines lean waiting for the order to reproduce. Behind them, pollarded willows and cypresses are intended to suggest normalcy, even intimacy in the ways they're shaped. Scattered here and there, butterflies float so still they look painted. As for me, as evening light fades I'll join others at the station or at the casino's back door, silent, as if each of us was a lost reference to someone else, nothing but nuance standing in a kind of light seen only at margins or borders, creeping away, or on walks that serve as entertainment where we can glimpse the afterimage of shadows, as lovely as we want to make them, as richly monochromatic as the motives of saints in a world seen clearest and most poignant in the leaving.

Painted Lady; or, Words in Air

Proust wrote in bed, Victor Hugo in a scratchy wool bodystocking, Winston Churchill wrote standing up, and I write on a slippery heap of tailings on the side of what remains of a mined-out mountain. It is hard to keep my footing, even harder to make notes and turn them into useful sentences. Everything is so quiet here. It's almost as if I can hear the scraping of thin grass blades, fritter of skinny weed stalks, trickle of dust. I can see light hiding in rock-shadows, drifting in pockets, creeping about. There are rock piles but no wind to cut on their edges, no breeze to calm thoughts. The mind droops, dips, viral like the time it lives in, the whole body nervous as conflicting winds, heart like a trapped bird as I try to keep my balance on shifting shale, finding it hard to move. There's nowhere to go, I think, just as I catch a glimpse of something that may not be there, a young woman among the rocks, naked as a rock, wrestling a snake while a crowd like sparrows presses round. My feet slip from under me again. It's drizzling. I want to say something, but decide to write it on the damp air, inscribing gestures I'll collect later. On air I apologize for my shortcomings, my failures. I'm sorry for everything, I write. No need to elaborate. I am afraid of dying. As I look out over the ravaged mountainside, stones turned at all angles, heaped and broken, I see as if framed me, myself, struggling uphill in our old pasture's mud, trying to catch up with my father who is pushing an empty wheelbarrow. Look at that Naked Lady, he says, pointing to a bedraggled butterfly. Painted Lady, I say to myself, afraid to correct but imagining my words on paper where they'd feel most real, almost something to rely on.

The Debate

Swathed, she was, from top to toe, like the Arab woman I saw decades ago in Ashkelon, swathed in black, weighed down with sacks and packages, staggering along in the gutter, trying to keep up with her husband who strode ahead on the sidewalk, rifle slung across his shoulders, never looking back. I entered the post office behind her, then stood in line on the plastic footprints keeping us the required six feet apart. She hooked her cane on the counter edge and rummaged with both hands in her large bag until it was her turn to go to the window. But she forgot her cane. Muffled by my mask, "Miss," I called, not knowing what else to call her. "Miss!" Faces turned to me. "No," I mumbled, "I meant *that* Miss." But that miss was almost at the window before she stopped, turned, glared at me, came back and snatched the stick. I must have reminded her of her incapacity. No wonder she was angry.

    I was thinking about this as I walked down the street increasingly lively with people coming out of hiding, until something made me look back quickly to my right. A pool of water left by last night's cold rain in the gutter was following me. Mm, I thought, continuing on my way, as if I hadn't noticed it. But quickly, I looked back again, and there it was still. So what? I thought, my attention diverted by the necessity of having to step over a large black ant crossing my path. He seemed so alone, surrounded by what—well, what was it all to an ant? Nothing, or close to. How could he know where he was, so small in such vastness? I would have liked to have done more for him, remembering, when things were normal, how small I'd felt high on that cliff face at the mouth of a cave. Waiting for the debate to begin, I'd looked down at two ponds, side by side, dug out of the wetlands where as a kid I used to listen to frogs. Now one pond was full of baby trout, not a good idea since trout need living, quick water, while the other had what seemed like lazy large carp and what appeared to be a dead frog floating belly-up, white. I looked across to the other cliff with a building on top where, recognizable by Bermuda shorts, t-shirt and backpack, the American lecturer came out through one door, looked about, said something, and went back in through the other. The Englishman in suit and tie, came out through the door the American had just entered, looked about, said something, and exited via the door the American had entered by. The debate was about to begin. I looked round at my colleagues, none of whom I liked, and none liked me. They were all historians with varying views of the past. "Look," I said, "a frog!" "A *dead* frog," said one of my colleagues. "You don't know that," added another. They all laughed and began discussing the way in which one could or could not know. The debate across the way had begun, but since the sound didn't cross the divide, they all decided to get closer. History, I was thinking as I watched them climb down via the rope ladder, descend unsteadily the thin geological layers until they disappeared along the valley floor, history is what we'll never get used to. It's always catching up and overtaking us, rushing on ahead, never standing still, so how can we examine it? As I looked out, I envisioned Plato and the blurred outlines of his cave wall, people bumping into and falling over each other in the dark, not an orderly process at all. But perhaps I was missing something, so I too decided to descend via the rope ladder and rope handrail, past the different colored layers, until I arrived on the unstable talis, righted myself, and took a breath. I looked to the end of the valley where another cliff sloped gently from left to right and

I saw coming down, outlined, silhouetted against the bright western sky, like articulated cut-out puppets and figures in a shadow play or a Javanese wayang theater, an unmoving line of horses and carriages, all black, riders and coachmen pulling reins taut, horses' legs braced against the descent. They may have been stationary but they were going full tilt, such was the artistry, such was the skill. The longer I watched, the faster they moved, the stiller they were. I was glad I'd learned to trust my eyes with their saccadic movements skipping and jumping as they constructed a world as much nothing as anything.

Brian Swann

You Never Know

A trench dug deep and long in what had been an abandoned industrial site. Along the trench stretched a wing-shaped construction in process of being raised on end. Fully hoisted, it was revealed to be tall, rising to a point. Something like skin stretched over it so thin you could see right through vein-like lines, filaments and filigree of cross-hatched bars, pencil-thin beams. It looked fragile, but also appeared resilient and taut, like a sail, the whole thing quivering in the breeze, echoing, reverberating. What could be the purpose of this, so out of date, so atavistic and one might even say redundant, perhaps left over from another age? Could it be a wing reconstituted from a gigantic extinct insect, one in the process of evolving into—what? Science, my friend reminded me again, invents things before there is any purpose or need. But it might come in useful in ways we can't even imagine. Or it may never have any use at all. You never know, he said. Things change so fast it might prove a vital corrective. To what? I asked. Just what it is itself, he replied. He paused to let this sink in, then turned and headed back down the path that had brought us here, leaving me in front of a wall of field stones piled up a few centuries back by men and oxen who cleared these forests. Now the trees had all come back, denser and darker. Here and there stones had toppled, or shaken loose, piled up at various angles. I squeezed through a gap into dense scrub and undergrowth, looking for the path. The Indians, I said to myself, would have had all this burned off and cleared but, I added, see how far that got them. I had been on the road since March, when the virus struck. It was now into the new year. What's up next? I wondered. You never know, I replied.

Odyssey

I am wandering about in my head: Covid, covert, cavort, cover-story, covert, the hidden— but how much this pandemic has revealed on all levels, social, psychological, you name it, memories forgotten, subverted, submerged, sublimated, invented. I meander, I ignore or by-pass. What else is there to do in a time for which you don't want to be held responsible? I sit at evening in this deep Prussian-blue sofa, haunted by thoughts like sudden allergies and ghosts' pricks, pulses in the wrist. There's a blue notebook beside me in which I write thoughts and quotations such as "when we reflect on the manifold manifestations of memory the mundane becomes marvelous," Jerome Groopman. Yes, the marvelous. It once stood for great things, prodigal with ideas borrowed and home-grown. Blue is my favorite color, though sometimes ash-blue becomes the shadow of a woman's hands on the windowsill there where, outside, coltsfoot is the yellow of silence. But blue is not so innocent when it is the result of Prussian blue mixed with sulfuric acid to produce hydrogen cyanide aka prussic acid, that very Zyklon B which left its glorious blue residue on the bricks at Auschwitz. Now the mind takes off in the wrong direction. I pull it back to where I sit on the lovely, plush Prussian-blue sofa under an oar I've taken with me on my wanderings since college days. I'm remembering the man I met in Paris who left Harlem to trace the journeys of Richard Wright across Europe. He was lugging along with him the large desk on which Wright wrote *Native Son*, and, the man claimed, *Black Boy*. Memory, memory. I do not care if one day's larger than another or if in my mind a psalm from boyhood dissolves into the cries of seabirds I remember as yesterday. But today I need to get a grip, since a floor is being added to my house, and a new set of stairs. I sit back and look at what has been accomplished so far. I am particularly anxious about the landscape canvasses I had ordered to match the scenes outside the house and which are late being delivered. I try to create in my mind the effects I had anticipated by their placement, deep satisfaction at the details and inner coherence. But this will only bring pleasure for so long and my stopgap will soon seem flimsy, leaving a man frightened by his own thoughts and memories, such as the time I was winding my way home one evening and passing a shadow in a dark doorway, hearing it say something like *nothing explains the improbable*. I looked about, then up at a line of birds like a disembodied arm, or a disembodied arm waving like a line of birds, which scared me, I don't know why, perhaps that the improbable evades meaning, and much in our lives is improbable.

    Yes, I need that floor and those stairs, and those paintings. But just as I hear what I think is the doorbell, I hear someone say "Forgive me." I look about. No one, not even someone delivering those tardy landscape paintings. But it gets me to wonder about sin and forgiveness and poor old Odysseus, the wanderer, forcing me wonder if I could forgive those responsible for delivering the impossibly tardy landscape paintings. What did Odysseus do to so anger Poseidon? All he did was blind the god's monster son who was eating his men. Neither Poseidon's initial anger nor his final appeasement made much sense to me. But such is the world, then and now which, I take it, is something like what the Buddha meant when he said to understand all is to forgive all, which, in my sick state moderated by Advil and Laphroiag, leads me to see snow falling across the zendo windows, *the tree reaching its branches*, me having a hard time, just sitting, the mind let loose, digging like a dog, sniffing its own self, battling cold contraries, but *not to understand the self, but to forget the self.* To forget you must once have known. I need to know. More snow is beating against the window. A bell rings. I lie on the old mattress on the monastery floor, covered with blankets the cat crapped on. *Lice, fleas,/the horse pissing/beside my pillow.* Beside the dead radiator I hear snow falling. *A mirror just reflects a dog's droppings, and when we remove those no stain is left on the mirror. And then it reflects a beautiful flower. When we remove the flower....* I can just make out my cloth arms and legs draped over my room's wooden chair like a boneless body. The mind goes to white blossoms on the picnic table. A dog howls as if he's flying. Noon brings snow and Albert who gets off his bike, red faced and apologetic. In half a dozen languages he asks his way home. I point, all the time eyeing the steaming compost pile topped with dry chrysanthemum flower-heads and think: If space is time and time space why don't they cancel out? That conundrum would help account for Albert's confusion, and my sense that I am everywhere and nowhere, standing aside, watching "myself" slide through simultaneous seasons, becoming everyone and no one, the way Albert is Albert and not Albert, there and not there. Which brings me to the blurry shadows of what could be the Ukraine, a wooden porch where I rest my oar and look out to one tall tree in the distance. "Poplar," I say, though I know it isn't, and beyond that a mud flat, "beautiful," I say, though it isn't. I just say this because someone could be watching or listening and I don't want to appear clueless or impolite. I keep to myself the fact that the poplar I'm sure is really a cottonwood, the kind that had once tricked me when I woke one May morning to find everywhere covered with what appeared to be snow. Just then I hear cries for help and look back to see a child thrashing about in the water. I rush over, save her, and become the hero of the hour, honored with bitter black coffee, almonds, and cuts of roasted meat which, though choice, lack a certain savor without salt. In return for their kindness, before picking up my oar and heading out into dark, I decide to trace for them on bark-paper the outline of a star reflected in a mirror, part of my navigational toolkit. It comes out backwards, of course, but how are they to know? They are very impressed, so on another sheet I draw the poplar and the mud flat stretching out until it can no more and the sea itself takes over and keep on going until it falls off the edge, where the sky also quits like a cigarette butt, and clicks shut like a deadbolt. They all look at me in wonder, everywhere goes quiet, as quiet, I remember, as when my grandmother one hot August afternoon ran cold water from the faucet over my wrists. I thank them, pick up my oar, and am about to leave when an elderly man asks, "We've been meaning to ask, but why do you carry that winnowing fan with you?" I walk a long time, then stop and plant the oar in the earth. I'll stay here. As you arrive at old age, you see what had been invisible but still nothing much seems real. That's the best I can do, so let's change the subject.

Beer and Bacon Sandwich

It isn't often one is in a position to look back over one's life and say definitively what were its happiest moments. This can only be done when the door is about to close but still ajar. My happiest moments were, one, holding a tall glass of golden beer up to light streaming in the window from a landscape covered with a heavy fall of snow, and two, in early summer standing on the lawn with a thick sandwich of white bread filled with bacon, biting deep into it. But, you might say—well, there are many things you might say, but the truth is the truth. A whole life can come down to a glass of beer and a bacon sandwich, and not just because for some time now I have now been forbidden both.

I had started to think like this on the way to visit an old friend, when, passing a bar, I caught a whiff of stale beer. These thoughts were still with me as, leaning on my cane, I stood in front of his very large painting. It was abstract, yet the closer I came I could make out, as from above, a kind of cityscape narrative, stretched and distorted somewhat in the manner of Francis Bacon. My friend, whose name was Piero Rande, had been a novelist but in later life had decided to be a painter since, he said, it afforded more freedom. He was searching his loft now for a smaller painting to fit exactly into the rear of the large one, make it more sturdy, he explained, a complete whole, like a box, looking forward and back at the same time, Janus-like. I felt like telling him this ambition seemed more appropriate for an avant-garde work of fiction, but held my tongue, and instead praised his painting and his ambition, though I did inquire who had painted the small painting. "I did, of course," he said. "Only I know what goes back there." To make up for my insensitivity, I pointed to a rather blank section high in the large painting.

"Yes," he said, "it needs something there." I was about to suggest something, when he said, "aren't you painting these days?" "Oh," I replied, "not for some time. I am not a painter. I just read about them and enjoy their company. However, recently I did sit a whole day in Jack's studio watching him paint *The Very Last Fish*." I paused. "Well," I ventured, "I have been painting a bit, more or less in the manner of Monet, or Manet, I can never quite tell the difference." "I'm sure they're quite stunning," he said kindly, sitting on the wood floor and looking out the window into the town's gray evening light. "They say," he said after a while, "that as you grow close to death you dream a lot." "I thought that was what they said about Covid?" "Maybe both," he said, "It's becoming harder for me to distinguish between the two." He labored to his feet. "You'd better leave now," he said, "it's getting dark." We moved toward the door. "Do you know the story 'Man Carrying Thing'?" "No, no, not really." "It's about indeterminacy, how the parts don't add up and the whole plays against them." "Oh, neat," I said, not knowing what else to say, thinking I would rather be someone else. My friend was staring at the ceiling. There should be much more to all this, I said to myself, and there may be more but not enough time to say it.

Time

I lie in bed after two jabs which I hope will save my life at least for a while until natural processes take their course and do their job with, for example, a heart attack which I've been promised for some time. My head aches thinking this at a time when time seems at once to stand still and stay the same, though there's still a lot to go, perhaps. Yes, there was a time when we got to pull down the sky and put it up again, be headlong in love with anything, no questions asked, but that was then. Now I do what I can with what's left which may not be enough. Today I felt like dragging myself out and administering a sound beating for all my failings, shortcomings, and sins. I remember the little monkey my Uncle Harry brought me back from the oil fields of Abadan, how he must have sensed something wrong with me even back then, for when he caught a glimpse of me, he screamed, jumped up on the mantelpiece, shat into his right hand and, not even bothering to aim, hit me every time. Which was bad enough, but not as bad as what happened to the poor cricket last summer. From a deckchair, I'd watched him being pushed and pulled up the cedar siding of our house by a wasp who got halfway to the top before both fell back down. Up again, down again, up, down, up, down. I closed my eyes under a sky so clear I could see right through to the other side where a wasp was pushing and pulling a cricket up a wall, only now I could hear the wasp's curses and grunts and the cricket's cries and screams. I open my eyes. This makes no sense. How come I remember this word for word? I want to make sense. Do I need to re-focus, change direction? How I got here's a mystery, but even the wind doesn't know where it's going especially when it gets there, so why should I? What's the quickest way to get anywhere? A straight line, mathematics. My father said I'd get nowhere without it and tried to beat it into me. "You're nobody. You'll get nowhere." So I got nowhere, but nowhere's not such a bad place. At least you know where you are. Still, I should have laughed in his face. Instead, I sang myself to sleep with a song to God the Father who never laughs and his Son who never cracked a smile. I hope God the Coder will show me how to get where I'm going because His numbers come out right much of the time even as He works on a better algorithm to pull everything together the way He drew it up before the Big Bang blew up in His face, smashing everything to smithereens so He had to start again thinking up excuses like fractals, integer sequences and other symmetry for us to believe in, keep us occupied while He starts again from the beginning, trying to figure out what went wrong, thus proving He exists, even if not why, thereby having the last laugh of his favorite joke whose punch-line is "Time."

The Idea of Progress

OK. Time, "that makes all and unfolds error," brings me in a heatwave almost to the second fall of leaf since the horror started, here and now where the manner in which people are responding to the Covid Delta variant is screwing up what's left of the Enlightenment and continuing Trump's destructive legacy. Yes, he's living up to his name from the Gothic and related to Swedish *trumpen*, "surly," and *trumpe*, "surly person." The word is even related to the reeve in Chaucer's eponymous tale set in Trumpington ("the tun of Trumpa's people") a man who is described as old, choleric and bitter. But enough diversion. On the TV news today I heard a man say he preferred death to being forced to wear a mask and a teacher at a rally furious at being deprived of her First Amendment right. "You mean," asked the interviewer, "that you're giving up the job you've done for twenty years if you're forced to get vaccinated?" "Absolutely," she replied, "it's a question of taking personal responsibility which is what we teach our children every day and to respect our autonomy and freedoms. We're Americans!" From behind her came "USA! USA! USA!" I also see that others in fantasy land are taking a drug called ivermectin which is intended to deworm cattle and horses. There are others who confuse the brain-wave delta with the Covid variation delta, claiming the vaccine puts you "under a spell" in a deep sleep "where you're not yourself," and still others who insist that the needle injects microchips into you—and so it goes on. The Idea of Progress. Ha! (I once visited the grave of J. B. Bury, he of *The Idea of Progress*, in the Protestant Cemetery in Rome. It was very overgrown). Did I mention Trump's suggestion that we should try using UV rays and the injection of disinfectant, "almost a cleansing"? It's a battle between science and reason on the one hand, and on the other the ancient human brain. We'll have to wait to see who wins. Maybe no one. Perhaps the dichotomy isn't so clearcut. Perhaps Goya realized this when, on his etching of a man sleeping on a paper-strewn desk he placed a caption: *El sueño de la razón produce monstruous,* which is usually interpreted as an expression of faith in Enlightenment values: The sleep of reason brings forth monsters. But in Spanish *sueño* can mean both "sleep" and "dream." Reason itself can generate monsters, not because it isn't awake to deal with them but because reason sleeping can actually create them; they are a consequence of reason, not in despite of reason. If so, how safe are we? Reason and science can produce wonders and horrors, perhaps in equal measure. History has plenty of examples and proof. Oh, well, who knows? Me, I can't wait for my Moderna booster to arrive, and until then I'm going to divert and protect myself with one final piece of disguised autobiography, real history, outright lies and fantasy. So "let be finale of seem," as long as one remembers that *being* is itself a game, no matter how serious. Yes, let it be, but first, or finally, I need to bring everything up to date.

During Covid, I'd chosen to stay indoors as much as possible, right deep into this hot, humid, sticky disgusting tropical summer, the hottest on record. But today I decided it was time to venture out for a walk (more like a slo-mo hobble) around my East Village neighborhood, just to see what had been happening during my absence. I chose morning, early, before crowds and traffic could cover it all up. And now I wish I hadn't. The place was a time-warp back to NYC in the late seventies and early eighties. Dog shit was everywhere, garbage piled up on sidewalks and in gutters, bus shelters were taken over by the homeless, the derelict, the unstable and purely insane. Others had camped out, plugged in, often on a mattress, around the LINK NYC free WIFI kiosks. Still others had found pleasant accommodations among tables, chairs, and plastic plants in sidewalk dining shacks. Here and there, on shop window walls, doors, anywhere, someone in a Magrittean moment had written THIS IS NOT REAL. All sorts of madness was roaming the streets, silent or shrieking, cursing, laughing, talking to themselves. I got back into air-conditioning as soon as I could, just in time for Hurricane Ira's tropical storm tail-wag to bear down on the city with a record deluge, catastrophic flooding, a twister or two, black-out and death. Perhaps, I thought, as I tried to revive a sputtering a/c and reboot the TV, being is not so much a game as a tactic, or tactics for survival. In any case, the best I can do now is to say with Natasha at the end of *Alphaville*, "*Je vous aime*," and hope for the best with, as I said, disguised autobiography, real history, outright fabrication, lies, fantasy. It's the best I can do.

Yes, the best I can do, more or less, like when I cannot get to sleep, e.g., last night, and again I tried imagining a world without humans, wiped out in a universal epidemic, all gone except for a few, including me, the old world returning new, as in the Ghost Dance, before I realized that this wouldn't work, for many reasons, and I returned to remotest Yukon or Alaska, with my huskies Muninn and Huginn, entering the log-cabin I'd built by hand and settling in, all three of us vegetarian so as not to disturb quail or caribou. We wander about wilderness wonders by day, and at night, by candlelight, I write about them. There is no sickness and no injuries, but of course something always halts this sleep-inducing tactic; it fails and I try the end of humanity again. Last evening, for example, I'd been reading, or trying to read, Foucault's *The Order of Things*, which ends with mankind being erased "like a face being drawn in sand at the edge of the sea," at which prospect the author feels "profound relief." As I lay thinking about this, however, I decided I'd need the sea itself to be erased for me to feel that same relief, because if it keeps on going in its old-fashioned way yes, the face would be erased, but another could be drawn after the sea retreats; erasure and renewal, something like Noah's Ark, and I didn't want that. So, rather than helping me get to sleep, these thoughts made my prospect even more remote, especially as I went on to contemplate all the plastic in the ocean and in our very blood, then how to stop the phosphorus that makes rich crops and our very bones from blooming in run-off and killing ponds, streams, lakes, the ocean itself and hence us, and how we might resolve all this by turning into machines, software hard and soft, non-human "minds" shooting off to stars.... And, yes, all this worked. Exhausted, I fell asleep to the tune of rain on the windows, pinging the AC....

Tintinnabulation

After a horrific cold that started over Thanksgiving and has gone well into the New Year, complete with a deep, hacking cough that's never stopped, constant throat-clearing as if preparing for an important speech, and Covid symptoms that turned out not to be Covid, I developed tinnitus, a sound like steam escaping or a cricket tapping out Morse code. Then came a blocked eustachian tube with a constant high-pitched scream higher than high C, in fact as if I was on the high seas in an old sailing ship, timbers creaking, groaning and popping. Sometimes it's even like Diamanda Galas at her best, or worst. When I speak now, my voice seems to bounce around inside my skull, muffled as if someone is mumbling in my head. With no cure, like life itself, it makes me long for sleep where, even if the noise continues, I can't hear it. To let my poor wife get some sleep, I kip in the living-room but most of the night I'm in my study trying to block out the noise in my ears with the noise on the page as I scratch on notepads or flip about in old notebooks, files, journals, scraps of paper. I don't find much, but I did come across a few sentences recently which I developed into something I called "Miss May, 1970." Out of curiosity, I tried to discover, via the vast resources of the internet, what happened to the lady in question but came up with nothing. She was certainly not the expert in cognitive theory at Harvard, nor the lady from Hickory Falls in Catabwa County whose obituary I read. In any case, whoever she is now, if anyone, or wherever, if anywhere, I wrote her story, about a woman who was a *Playboy* centerfold and whose friend had two vaginas.

*

I am hoping I'd have time to write up more of these narratives before the noise in my ears increases and drives me mad like poor Jonathan Swift whose auricular roaring and banging produced terrible vertigo such that he had "neither spirits to write, or read, or think." They even put garlic drizzled with honey into his ears and phosphorus oil made from an apothecary's piss. I wish I had his guts and ability to turn this horror into comedy, as he did in *Gulliver's Travels* when the house which the giantess Glumdalclutch gave him is snatched up into the air by an eagle and all Gulliver can hear is "a Noise just over my Head like a clapping of Wings," along with bangs and buffets that sounded louder to his ears "than the Cataract of Niagara." But while I am still able, in a continuing effort to drown out the whistling and banging, the tintinnabulations of the bells, bells, bells, "the moaning and the groaning," as Poe put it, the sound of madness, in a short while I will append here a brief piece I've just completed called "The End of Art," if I can find it. It is pure fiction, though I recall once, after a poetry reading, overhearing someone ask Bill Merwin, "Was that a real poem, or did you make it up?"

Mother Esther of the Murmurations

Now there's no one here. Just me running a high temperature, again. The others, such as they are, are all gone, or in process of going, like the end of *The Cherry Orchard*. But that was in another place, another time that might as well never have existed for the past is strange, a collage, iron filings rearranging themselves round desire and accident, pulls and pushes of proof that have organized themselves to be themselves. Or the past dives about, on the run, seeking something, looking for you looking for it and there's a chance you'll meet, if only out of exhaustion, like the way I never married but always thought my wife could be somewhere, I didn't know where or what she could be doing. She could still be anything, anywhere.

Years ago, the day after I arrived not at this place but another, there, at my first job, I handed in my resignation after I'd been required to sign the savings and retirement forms that gave off death and made me panic. I was told not to read poetry on the job but I did. All they read were financial reports and balance sheets. I was so young and lonely in that northern city of red brick Victorian buildings, streets lit by orange lights, an oily ship canal running through built to import cotton grown on slave plantations and export goods made from said cotton. I'd chosen my address long distance by the sound of its name, Moss Lane. I'd imagined something like my childhood dairy, walls damp with bright green moss beside the churns, the smell of milk being ladled into glass bottles plugged with cardboard tops. But no. Moss Lane, since demolished for a multi-million stadium, had more in common with moss-troopers than moss walls, strumpets than milk-maidens. Still, I honored my commitment and stayed until my indenture was up, working as if I wasn't there. Then one day I looked up over the canal to a swirl, a twisting turning in and out like time itself, away and up, a susurration of almost Mozartian riffs and twirls interposing, intertwining into one symphonic thirl, a skirl, a ball, one being of many, moving away, leaving me longing. Starlings, they told me. Little stars.

Soon after I packed my cases, or rather my bag, my duffel bag stuffed with books and set off for a place I hadn't known existed. I decided to find myself in the dislocation of travel, and then lose myself whenever I had the chance in the fabric and fabrication of time.

Thus, after a long rough ocean crossing, unsure where I was and without even looking for her, I came upon Esther Wheelwright, "the little white flower," in Father Bigot's mission among the Abnaki, People of the Dawn, who had carried her off at the tender age of seven from Antinomian Wells. Luckily, a short while later she was redeemed to Quebec, thence to the Ursuline convent in Montreal where, a bride of Christ, she "took the white veil," refused repatriation, assuming a new name in a new language and religion, in a new place, becoming the first and last English Mother Superior. I felt a certain kinship. We were unique. I heard the mystic who lived in my duffel bag saying "lose the self to find the self." But first you had to find it.

Then in my solitary wanderings I lost her. Time passed, then more until I felt there was none left, and when I came upon her again she was no longer able to embroider, busying herself with mending the underclothing of the community with the same delicacy of darning and patching she'd shown with her beautiful handiwork or altar cloths, even while all around raged an epidemic of unusual ferocity, taking off the savages in droves. Yes, I watched her as if released beyond herself into colors of the weave that seemed to grow without need, working into what they were and leaving behind what was no longer needed. I thought I was watching a soul in the vestments, a vastness found there, a reverie swollen to fullness by the thrust of absence, I felt distance had made colors more sonorous in a new world that didn't really need to exist in ways I expected, grown from that little boat, that navicella "deeply laden with codfish" a long time ago, becoming the click of knitting needles, the draw of thread through cloth, the scratch of a pen such as this working on a map, making more clear who lived there or lives here, though now it's not clear anyone at all is here unless you count me who, with the distortion of influenza or yet another unknown virus brought to these shores, might be multiple or minimal as I look out the window at the murmuration of starlings over the Ursuline nunnery now a museum, admission free.

Brian Swann

Across the Wide Missouri

It's toward the end of the season, time to bring matters to an end. The girl in the cable-stitch sweater is on her way to feature as Pocahontas in the timeless spaghetti Western *The Marriage of the Trapper in the Open Air*. She is talking to the milord who is to play "old yeller hair" and to his lady who will be Sacajawea, complaining of having to be smeared with cochineal. They are waiting at the Missouri as the brass band plays "Shenandoah." The milord turns to give a group of locals mocking and loafing on the grass a V-sign with his right hand and a finger with his left. He will not be trifled with in what he refers to as "these red wastes." His bride of but a few weeks squints up at the station clock then down the tracks to look for the westbound train, the "gravy train" as the rude mechanicals call it, but the eastbound train comes first and pulls up in front of the obsolete open-sided crematorium where four bodies are waiting to be boarded, along with a number of crates headed back to Washington filled with all sorts of stuff which, according to lists appended and notices nailed to the sides turn out to be: assorted animals, dead and alive, whole and in part, Crow medicine bundles, lightly used, a collection of Ghost Dance shirts and deerskin dresses stained and pierced with bullet holes, fringed saddle decorations carefully made from pudenda cut out and stretched, along with a few choice tobacco pouches made from savage scrotums, all courtesy of one Colonel John Chivington. Scattered around and about said crates are bundles from which poke out a moccasin here, a fur robe there, a mat, a wooden spoon, a small bow made of bone, all sorts of treasures scavenged, no doubt, from the multitudinous recipients of the small-pox and other instruments destined, they say, by the spontaneous working of principles in the natural flow of events, to civilize "these red wastes," and beyond, with the sweep of our eagle's wings. Meanwhile, however, at the other end of town, a young man in a puffy red jacket who had insisted on going to the football game in high heels has encountered some difficulties in a bar and has had to fight his way out, in the process discovering that running in pumps presents its own problems, while in another flashback federal agents are interrogating wedding guests, and in yet another the groom has put Franz Lehar waltzes on the turntable which refuses to turn until he kicks it so everyone in period costume can begin to dance to the strict time-signature, except for the bride who is dumbly smoking a pipe and sulking because she does not approve of his choice of furrin music. Meanwhile the young man in heels and puffy jacket is still in a state of confusion as he high-tails it out of another bar thinking that all he wants is to be himself. And then the westbound train arrives. People get off, more get on, and the brass band begins to play vigorously so the sound almost drowns out the noise of coming and going on the banks of the wide Missouri, drifting away into the land of "settlement and civilization," forever for ever, where the sun never sets and *Ya-honk!* goes the wild gander.

Acknowledgments

"That's Life" appeared in *The Hudson Review* and "Across the Wide Missouri" appeared in *Plume*.

About the Author

BRIAN SWANN was born in Wallsend, England. He received his BA and MA from Queens' College, Cambridge, and his PhD from Princeton. He has published a historical novel, *Huskanaw* (Mad Hat Press, 2022), and many collections of poetry, the latest of which is *Imago*, (Johns Hopkins University Press, 2023)), as well as volumes of poetry in translation, short fiction, children's books, and has editing a dozen books of and on Native American literature. He has won a number of awards, prizes, fellowships, and lives in Manhattan with his wife the poet Roberta Swann (*Crack in the Door*, MadHat Press, 2017.) He taught at the Cooper Union until his retirement in 2022.